Indian Silversmithing

Indian Silversmithing

W. Ben. Hunt

ECHO POINT BOOKS & MEDIA, LLC
Brattleboro, Vermont

Published in 2022 by Echo Point Books & Media
Brattleboro, Vermont
www.EchoPointBooks.com

Indian Silversmithing
ISBN: 978-1-64837-257-5 (casebound)
978-1-64837-262-9 (paperback)

Cover design by Kaitlyn Whitaker

Front cover images: *Top*—Squash Blossom Necklace by alacatr, courtesy of iStock
Bottom: Antique Native American Sterling Silver Cuff by digitalfarmer, courtesy of iStock
Back cover illustrations: from the book

Contents

Foreword	5
Introduction	7
Tools and Equipment	9
Punches	14
Silver Soldering	19
Silver	23
Concha Buttons	25
Money Clips	31
Tie Clasps and Hair Clips	33
Lapel Pins and Brooches	34
Rings Without Settings	39
Tarnishing or Antiquing	45
Heating and Soldering Frames	45
Turquoise in Indian Jewelry	46
Polishing Turquoise	51
Silver Bezels	56
Rings Set With Turquoise	60
Men's Rings	65
Channel Work	69
Ear Ornaments	71
Brooches	77
Concha Belts	79
Neckerchief Slides	83
Katcina Neckerchief Slide	87
Appliqué Work	89

PILL AND STAMP BOXES	91
OVAL AND ROUND SALTCELLARS	93
BRACELETS OF SHEET SILVER	95
BRACELETS OF HAMMERED SILVER	103
ARM GUARDS OR KETOS	109
BELT BUCKLES	114
BELT-BUCKLE SETS	121
ANTIQUE TEA STEEPER	125
UNIQUE BROOCHES	127
DRAGONFLY BROOCH	131
LAPEL PINS	133
TURQUOISE TURTLE PIN	137
SQUASH-BLOSSOM NECKLACES	138
HOLLOW SILVER BEADS	138
SQUASH BLOSSOMS	142
PENDANTS	145
STRINGING BEADS	145
WRIST-WATCH BANDS	148
MINIATURE VASES AND CANTEENS	151
EMERY POLISHING STICK	154
IMPORTANCE OF THE SKETCHBOOK	157
INDEX	159
COLOR ILLUSTRATIONS	
BRACELETS, BROOCHES & PINS	FACING PAGE 64
BELT BUCKLES	FACING PAGE 65
RINGS, BUTTONS, NECKLACES, PINS	FACING PAGE 80
TURQUOISE AND CRYSOCOLA	FACING PAGE 81
AUTHOR BIOGRAPHY	161

A Short History of Native American Silversmithing in the Southwest

THE ART of silver jewelry making in the American Southwest began over a century and a half ago in the mid-1800s when Navajo blacksmith Atsidi Sani and his sons began producing a variety of useful silver products such as knives and bridle parts. Before long, they and others added items of handcrafted jewelry and other fine-art ornaments to their output. Prior to this, most jewelry and other ornaments in the region were made from shells, bones, and local semiprecious stones.

For early practitioners of silversmithing, necessary ingenuity led to fortuitous innovation. Smiths fashioned their stamps, shears, pliers, and other instruments of the trade from old metal tools and other implements obtained through trade. Soldering was often done directly in the coals of fires, with blowpipes adding extra heat. Silver itself was initially obtained by melting down silver coins, first from U.S. currency and then, after that became illegal, from Mexican coins. The art form continued to grow as each generation of smiths taught their skills to the next.

From the Navajo, the craft spread to neighboring groups, including Pueblo, Hopi, and Zuni tribes, with each introducing distinct styles and variations. These southwestern Native American tribes often traded among themselves at first, but two significant developments around the turn of the century brought changes to this simple arrangement.

The first change was an evolution of the art itself. Taking inspiration from historic use by Pueblo, Navajo, and other tribes, jewelry makers began setting the semiprecious gemstone turquoise into their pieces, and the practice only intensified as mining of turquoise increased. The use of turquoise with silver is now a hallmark of southwestern jewelry. The other development was the arrival of a burgeoning tourist trade in the region due to the expansion of the railroad and the establishment of trading posts. For the first time, items such as bracelets, necklaces, and conchos were now specifically made for and marketed to tourists for commercial consumption, as well as to other local artists and tradespeople.

The art of silversmithing continued to evolve over time, both technically and culturally. Initially, it was practiced only by men, but by the early 1920s women were learning the trade as well and soon became adept practitioners, increasing commercial output. Each tribal group refined its own unique, distinctive style, which, in modern culture, produces pieces ranging from bold to exquisitely delicate, allowing for a wide range of personal aesthetics.

When Ben Hunt first published *Indian Silversmithing* in 1952, little attention was paid to the terminology of its title. Hunt was noted for his deep respect for the people whose craft he researched and wrote about, and almost certainly would advocate today for the more respectful terms "Native American" or "Indigenous Peoples."

Referenced for generations, Hunt's *Indian Silversmithing* stands the test of time as a classic guide to the history and craft of silver jewelry making in the American Southwest. It offers a rich history of this much admired art form and provides an invaluable reference manual for enthusiastic crafters and hobbyists who want to learn and practice the craft themselves.

Introduction

SILVER as a medium for the craftsman's art is several centuries old, yet the art of silversmithing as practiced by the Navaho, Zuni, and other Pueblo Indians is relatively young. Old Spanish writings indicate that as early as 1795 "Navaho captains were rarely seen without their silver ornaments," but it was not until somewhere between 1850 and 1870 that the Navahos acquired the skill from the Mexican *plateros* (silversmiths). From the Navahos the art spread to the Zunis, and to a lesser degree to other smaller tribes of the Pueblo groups.

It is probable that no American craft has been more widely admired than silversmithing as practiced by the southwest Indians. Beauty and richness resulted from the weight and quality of silver, and the feeling for design, displayed by the *jeweler* working to please himself. His work carried aesthetic and religious values and was an investment comparable to our stocks and bonds, or diamonds.

Much of the Navaho jewelry available in department and ten-cent stores today is factory made. True, some of it is made by the Indians themselves, but from measured quantities of silver furnished by traders who expect the workers to turn out as many articles as possible. The result is the articles are thin and brittle, and sell at a low price. The character and design of the articles are also dictated by trade demands. Swastikas, arrows, and horses predominate in the cluttered patterns to which curio dealers have attributed symbolic meanings. However, this is sales promotion rather than fact.

For many years a student of Indian life and crafts, Ben Hunt has visited extensively among the southwest Indians, absorbing the skills of their artisans and their love of silver as a medium in which to work.

In INDIAN SILVERSMITHING, Ben Hunt offers the craftsman a series of adventures in the making of silver articles, some of which, like the Keto are authentic; others, like the saltcellar, are purely functional. In most instances, the decorations presented here are the native designs consisting of elementary geometrical forms which follow the contour of the articles and leave softly gleaming expanses of silver. A few others have been taken from designs used in rugs and pottery.

Believing firmly that more fun will be had in building from the ground up, and that more pride will result in the finished product, Mr. Hunt describes the making of many of the necessary tools. From this point, the text progresses naturally from the simple to the more complex project. Each section is similar to a job sheet complete with instructions, for each material, tool, or operation is introduced as the need arises. Drawings and photographs by the author make the various techniques or construction clear and easy to carry out. Whether the reader be a serious craftsman or merely one looking for a hobby, this book has much to offer.

LAWRENCE HALPENNY
Assistant Executive
Boy Scouts of America
Minneapolis, Minnesota

Tools and Equipment

THE words *Indian silversmithing* and *Navaho and Pueblo jewelry* bring visions of beautiful pieces of hand-wrought silver and turquoise jewelry to those who have seen this work. Rings, ear ornaments, bracelets, bow guards, necklaces, concha belts and buttons, belt buckles, and numerous other things are made in silver by the Indians in the southwestern part of our country. Many who have seen Indian silverwork have had a desire to try to make some. The white man can form silver, cut turquoise, and solder up the pieces, but the designs that are used by the Indians are their own. No two pieces of jewelry made by the Indians are exactly alike unless one thinks of a pair of ear ornaments, a concha belt, or a row of beads. Indians do not work in a production line. Therefore, a showcase full of identical pieces of silver and turquoise jewelry is not Indian made even though the tag says it is. This production jewelry probably has been assembled and soldered by Indians, but the different elements and parts of each piece were punched out by the thousands with white man's machinery.

In this book we do not intend to show how commercial jewelry is made, but rather how silversmithing is done in the hogans and pueblos on the reservations.

Rather than begin with instructions on how to make a piece of jewelry, the tools used by an old-time silversmith, in his hogan, will be discussed. An important piece of equipment is his forge, used to melt silver to be cast into ingots or molds. This consists of pieces of stone or broken pottery cemented together with adobe clay, equipped with a homemade bellows. A common gasoline blowtorch supplies the necessary heat for soldering. His anvil, most likely, is a section of rail or it may be any chunk of iron. An assortment of hand tools is used by the Indian, such as an old claw hammer or a machinist's hammer from some automobile tool kit, a pair of cheap pliers or two, and often, instead of a tin snips, a pair of old shears. A box usually contains an assortment of odd-shaped dies and punches made of whatever metal can be found. The dies are made

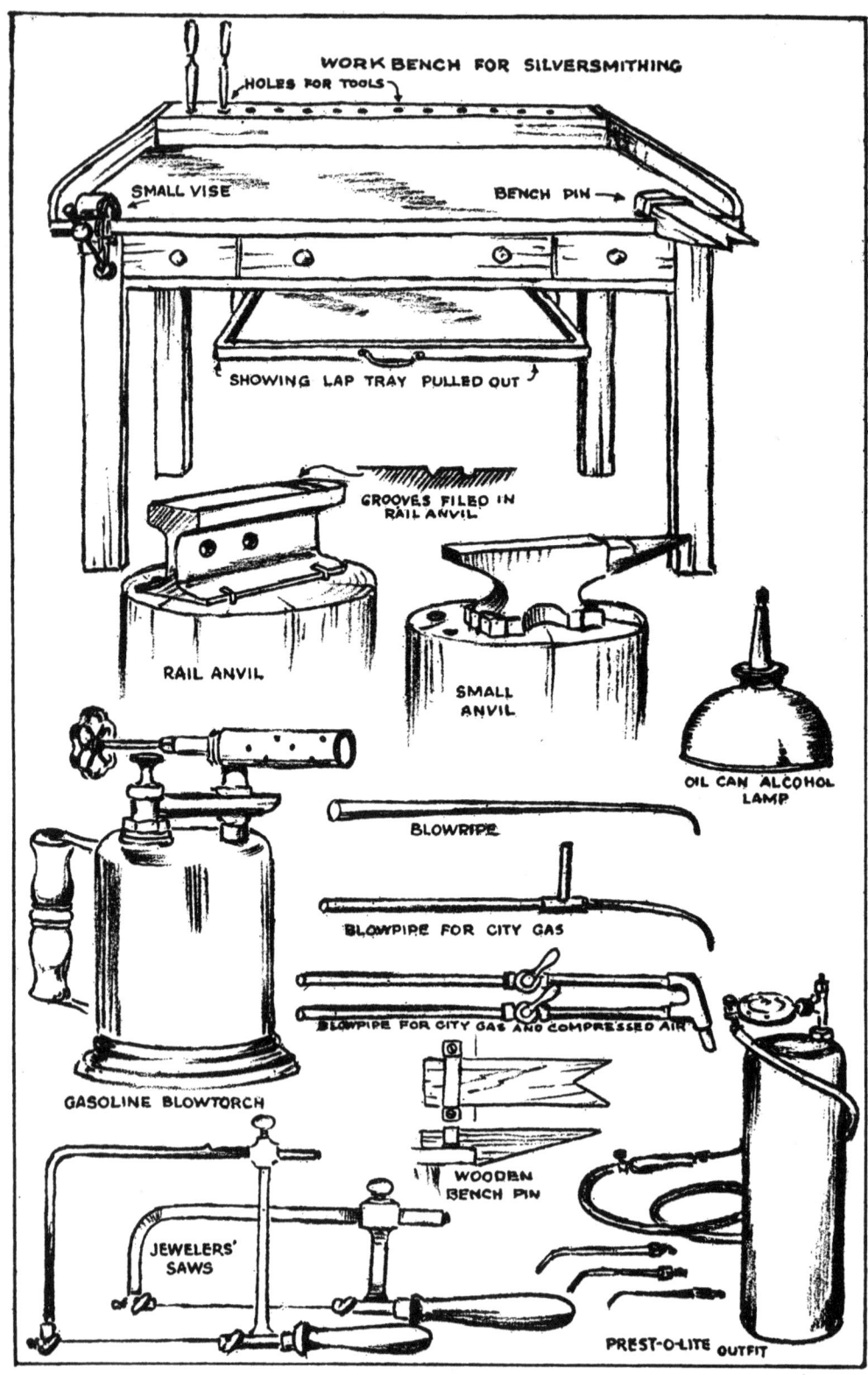

PLATE 1

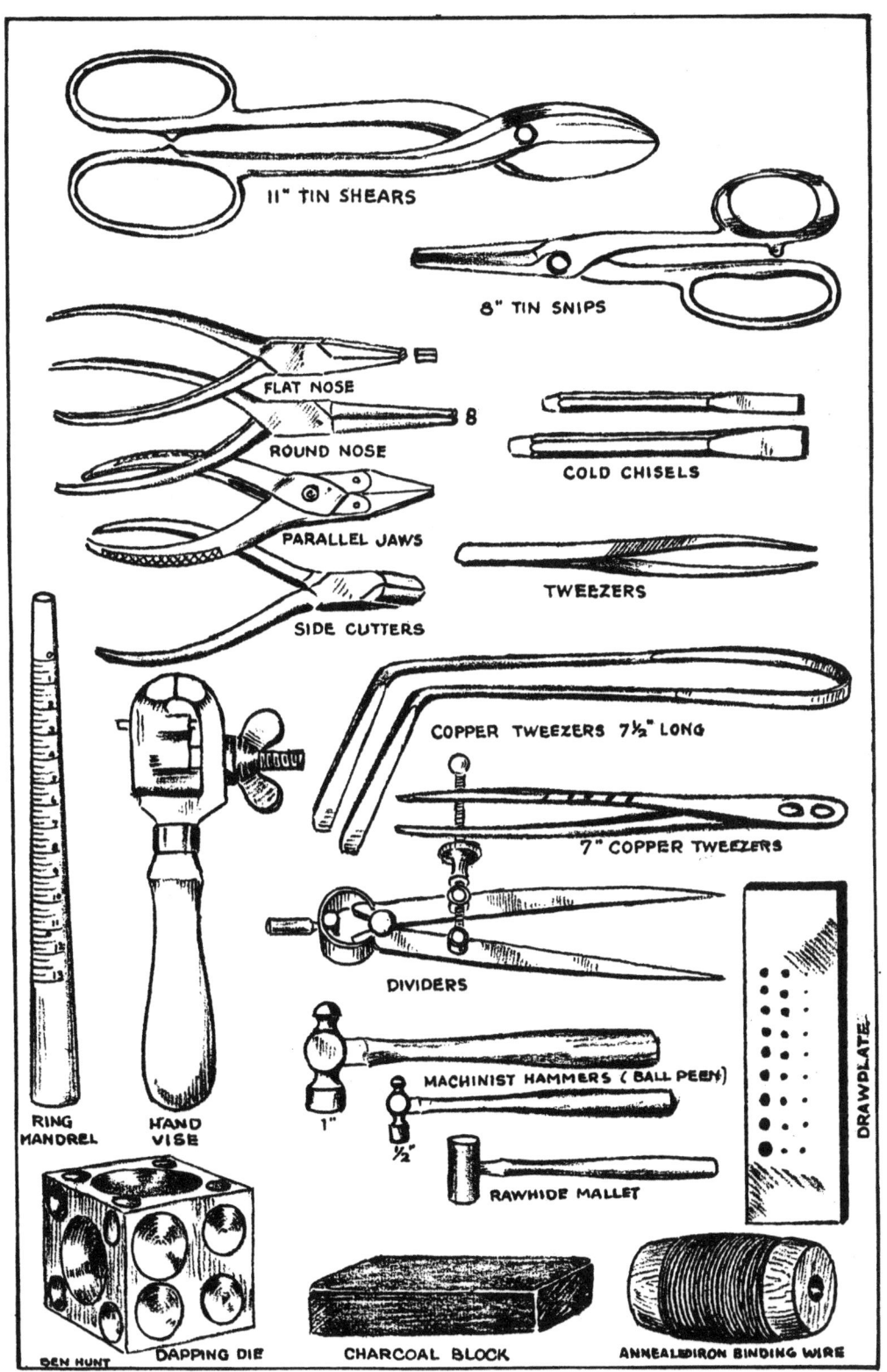

PLATE 2

by forging and filing down pieces of bolts or old files or any other metal pieces. This silversmith has a file or two and some emery cloth, and, all in all, it does not seem possible that he can turn out anything with so few tools. But, he makes use of anything he has at hand, first, because he can't stop in at a hardware store or a dime store every time he wants something, and, second, because he knows how to work with simple tools. As to ideas, he has many tucked away in his mind. That is an Indian trait — the storing up of ideas. The Navaho woman, for instance, uses her own ideas when she weaves the designs in her elaborate rugs.

The Indian silversmith, as a rule, figures out his designs according to the piece of turquoise and the amount of silver he has. The modern Indian has the same tools we use. The Navaho, however, who is a nomad and moves from one place to another to find pasturage for his sheep and horses, cannot burden himself with a lot of equipment. But, he can and will use any modern equipment he can obtain, and nothing pleases him more than a wire drawplate or good files or pliers.

A beginner in silversmithing should remember that it is not necessary to buy a lot of expensive equipment to start with. Some things are rather essential, but experience has shown that getting and making equipment and tools as they are needed is more gratifying than just buying a lot of things that probably never will be used. Remember that tools alone will not produce well-balanced and well-designed pieces of jewelry. For the first piece of jewelry, one of the bracelets shown in Plate 28 or 31 can be made, using nothing more than a mill file, a triangular file, and a chisel.

The first thing to do is to find a good spot for a workshop or work space. This space should be such that unfinished work can be left as is without being disturbed until it can be taken up again. The workshop also should have a cabinet to store small tools, and drawers for the silver, silver solder, and stones.

A solid table or bench is necessary, and a small 3- or 4-in. vise should be fastened to one side of it. In jewelry shops and in the Indian schools where silversmithing is taught, a sliding tray that can be pulled out over the worker's lap to catch chips and silver filings is located below the table. These scraps and filings accumulate to a surprising degree over a period of time. They should be put into a tin or wooden box until such a time when casting is to be done or when scrap is to be melted and rolled into sheets again. This tray need be only 1 in. deep, and it should have a tin or stainless-steel bottom. It is well to cover the entire top of the table with a sheet of metal or asbestos, because this is easily cleaned and holes will not be burned in the table when soldering.

The workshop also should have a shelf or a space on the wall for tools. A well-shaded 100-watt lamp should be above the workbench.

A necessary piece of equipment is an anvil. This can be a regular small anvil or a piece of rail. If it is a piece of rail, be sure it is not worn down. This wear usually is one-sided and on a slant. Get a new piece of rail, if possible, preferably a foot long. The anvil, no matter what kind it is, should be mounted on a block or log at least 12 in. in diameter, and at a height so that it can be used while seated. The space on the block or log not covered by the anvil will come in handy when shaping silver. Depressions can be cut or hammered into the log when needed, and a large log will stand more solidly than a small one.

A gasoline torch solves most of the heating problems. These torches are not expensive and are easy to handle and transport.

Fuel or illuminating gas and a small blowpipe as shown in Plate 1 also can be used. The use of blowpipes will be shown and described later.

For very small work, an alcohol lamp and blowpipe sometimes are used. This method of heating is not recommended for general work, however, nor are the small automatic blowtorches.

An ideal layout for soldering, melting, and annealing silver is a small portable gas tank equipped with hose and different size nozzles. Illuminating or fuel gas is the simplest form of heating. Portable gas such as Prestolite is second. It can be really called the ideal heating unit, since it is portable and does not require a blowpipe which sometimes is a nuisance. It also provides enough heat for melting silver in crucibles for small casting and can be used with a small nozzle or burner for very small work. Fuel or natural gas, if used with a double blowpipe and a small air compresser, also can be used for smelting. The drawback with a gasoline blowtorch is that it takes a while to light it and, unless the tiny openings are carbon free, it cannot be turned down to a low flame while not in use. Gas, on the other hand, can be shut off and on in an instant.

Several hammers will be required. If no hammers are among the tools, choose a medium-size, ball-peen machinist's hammer with a 1-in. flat face to begin with. Later, get a smaller hammer and probably a larger one for heavy work. Ball-peen hammers are ideal for Indian jewelry. The ball is useful in many ways.

Four tools can be used to cut silver, such as the cold chisel, the tin shears, the jeweler's saw, and the cutting pliers. The cold chisel is probably the simplest tool to use, but it cuts up the face of the anvil. Several small chisels also should be in the tool rack.

A good tin shears is a *must*. In fact, there should be two, a large one and a small one. A jeweler's saw comes in mighty handy at all times. Get one with an adjustable frame, if possible, and about 6 in. deep. An assortment of blades should be on hand, ranging from No. 2/0 to 1½ or 2. For use with the saw, a bench pin should be fastened to the bench over the tray to be used for both sawing and filing.

A great many types of pliers can be used for silversmithing. Flatnose pliers for flat work and roundnose pliers for wire will be found helpful. For cutting wire, parallel-jaw or side-cutting pliers are recommended. Never cut wire with tin shears.

Tweezers should be among the tools for handling the small snippets of solder and for assembling small work. It may be well to make the two shown in Plate 2. They are made of heavy copper wire and are very useful. A small hand vise also can be used in many ways.

An assortment of files is quite necessary. Files for jewelry work should be rather fine cut. A good flat file, a half-round and a round file are enough for the beginning. When making the more elaborate pieces, a set of needle files are required.

For shaping rings, a ring mandrel is necessary. This is a long tapered piece of round steel with ring sizes marked on it.

A small hand drill also should be provided.

For making hollow beads and hammering up half spheres, a dapping die will be helpful. The old-time Indians made these dies of hardwood and used a metal punch.

A rawhide hammer also is a good thing to have, but a small wooden mallet will do equally as well. A motor-driven grinding wheel with a felt or muslin polishing wheel on one side is useful, but if none is on hand, silver can be polished by hand with powdered pumice stone and crocus cloth.

The Indian and most white silversmiths make all or most of their die stamps. Die stamps are rather important in some of this work and more will be said later on about designs and how to make them.

Many small tools, such as center punches, scribers, dividers, and other tools can be obtained from time to time as they are found necessary.

A few charcoal blocks or a piece of asbestos will be needed for soldering. A 1-gal. stone jar can be used as a pickle jar for most work. A pyrex frying pan, heated on a gas burner or on a small electric heating unit, may be used for cleaning silver.

Some of these essential items should be on hand when beginning this silversmithing work. Other small items may be added from time to time.

Punches

Probably the most prized of all the Indian silversmith's possessions is his collection of punches which are used to stamp designs in silver. Their value lies in the fact that they are all handmade. They are not as a rule perfectly formed, and regardless of how many similar punches there are of the same design, being handmade, there are no two exactly alike. Nor is the metal of which they are made alike. A white man's collection of punches usually is uniform in many ways, because he can go to a dealer or hardware store, and buy the exact size and shape of steel he wants. Not so with the Indian. He makes his stamps out of steel or iron that he picks up here and there. Old iron buggy tires often are used. They have acquired a toughness from pounding over gravel and stony roads. A lot of the metal the Indian uses for dies is soft steel and iron, and he tries to harden it by heating it red hot and quenching it in cold water. Some pieces of steel, such as old files, become very brittle and glass hard with that treatment, while others acquire little or no hardness. But, the Indian somehow or other gets by with his simple tools,

FIG. 1. Handmade silversmithing tools

and produces jewelry that we, with all our modern and up-to-date equipment, can hardly hope to reproduce. It may be that we strive too much for perfection in small details, whereas the Indian looks at each piece as a whole. It seems that the imperfections in the jewelry produced by the Indian are so consistent that it really makes for more beautiful workmanship. This is true of nearly all Indian craftwork and is due to the fact that machine work does not enter into it in any way.

Some of the Indian's technique may be acquired by using tools and equipment similar to his. Therefore, material around the shop, not scrap iron exactly, but pieces of steel that are no longer useful for something else, may be made into such tools. Of course, excellent punches may be made out of $3/16$-, $7/64$-, $5/16$-, and $3/8$-in. diameter drill rod. Then, too, $1/4$- to $3/8$-in. cold chisels can be transformed into fine punches.

Plate 3 shows how to proceed in making punches out of cold chisels, some of which are of round stock and others of octagonal shape. Since the chisels have been tempered, they should be ground to shape on a power or hand grinding wheel, being careful not to burn them. Several straight punches can be made by simply shaping the edge as shown in

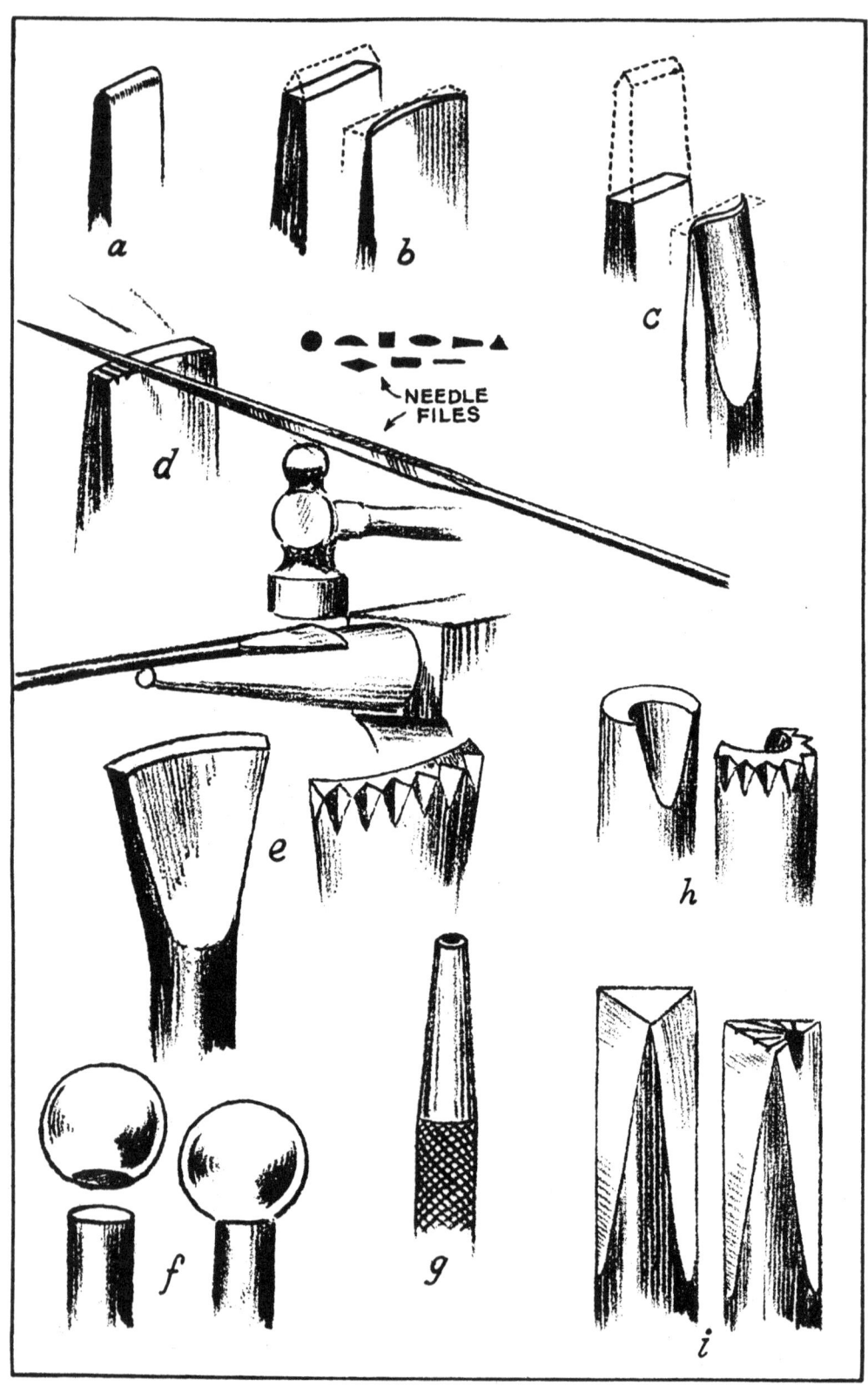

PLATE 3

PLATE 4

the enlarged sketch at *a*, Plate 3. This type of punch must be given a smooth, rounded, straight edge. Make three or four of these punches, ranging from 1/16 in. in width to the width of the widest chisel as shown in Plate 4. After these punches have been ground, smooth them with fine emery or carborundum cloth and oil. Then make a few curved punches shaped like those shown at *c*, Plate 4. First grind off the edge as shown at *b*, Plate 3, and then grind them to shape and finish with fine abrasive cloth and oil.

Compound curves used in stamping rope and leaf designs, as shown at *e*, Plate 4, and *c*, Plate 3, can be made in the same manner from small chisels, without changing their temper or hardness. Grinding the chisels on a power grinder calls for rather careful work but it saves a lot of time.

Also make several small diamond and triangular shapes like those in *f*, Plate 4. The shapes described so far can be made without annealing and retempering.

To produce the shapes shown at *h*, *i*, and *j*, Plate 4, first anneal the cold chisels. Annealing means taking out the temper. To do this, heat the cold chisel over a gas burner or blowtorch to a bright red, and then let the steel cool very slowly. Probably the best way to do this is to bury the heated steel in hot ashes until it cools off. After that, shape the steel with files. It is best to use needle files for this work. First, file the general shape and then the fine lines and triangles, etc., as shown at *d*, Plate 3. Drill rod, when purchased, is very soft and easily filed. To make some of the larger dies requires a bit of forging previous to filing. That is where the 3/8-in. rod comes in handy. Heat the rod with a gas flame, furnace, forge, or blowtorch, and hammer it to about the shape desired. Then file it to shape and harden and temper it.

To harden and temper a punch, heat the design end and about one half of the punch to a bright red. Then plunge the hot end into cold water. The design end of the punch now is hardened, while the other end is allowed to remain somewhat softer, and therefore tougher.

Next, rub the design end of the punch with a piece of emery cloth until it is bright. Then reheat the front end of the punch by moving it about in the flame of the blowtorch. Do not put the design itself into the flame, and watch the part that has been brightened with the emery cloth. First, a straw color will appear, then bronze, then a beautiful dark blue, and just as soon as this appears, plunge the whole punch into the water until it has cooled off fully. An Indian trader in the west tempered his tools by heating them to a bright red and dunking them in beeswax. This method has proved very satisfactory. Finish the punch with abrasive cloth and oil or on a buffing wheel. Be careful not to take off any of the fine corners and edges of the hardened punch. If you have no beeswax, dunk or quench the red-hot end in a can of cup grease.

Trying to stamp hard silver soon will ruin a soft-tempered punch unless the silver is annealed.

How to make a dapping punch is shown at *f*, Plate 3. Even though no dapping block is on hand, half-rounded sections or parts of jewelry can be hammered out with such a punch by working on a hard piece of end-grain wood, like the top of the log on which the anvil has been fastened. To make these small dapping punches, get an assortment of steel ball bearings measuring upward from $3/8$ in. to whatever diameter is desired. Then file or grind the end of a piece of steel rod to a flat section, grind a flat section on the ball bearing, and silver solder the ball to the rod. To do this soldering, set the piece of steel rod upright, and place the ball on the end of it (see "Silver Soldering," following). Plunge the punch into cold water immediately after the solder has set. Indians often use the ball of a ball-peen hammer if that is the size contour they wish to hammer up. The stamping punches shown in Plates 3 and 4 may be used to produce a great many designs. Stick to the simple dies that the Indian makes and uses, for better results.

Plate 4 shows a variety of punch designs for silverwork. Other designs may be added as required.

Also have an assortment of hollow nail sets of all sizes to make the designs shown in *g*, Plate 4. In Plate 3, *h* and *i* show how punches are filed out of round drill or other steel rods. The symbolic cow's head with the cactus spines in her nose, in Plate 4, is rather unusual in Indian silver stamping, but it is amusing and does not require any special punches.

The lower two rows of designs in Plate 4 are edges stamped on concha buttons and pins.

Silver Soldering

Silver soldering seems a little difficult until the knack of doing it has been acquired. Cutting out, sawing, bending, and forming can be done at leisure, while soldering is a job that must be completed in one operation. There are as many *don'ts* to soldering as there are *do's*. Probably the most important thing to remember is that the joint or parts to be soldered *must* be clean. There is no alternative to that. The parts of the metal where the solder is to adhere must be filed or scraped clean.

Use a flux for soldering silver the same as when joining tin or other sheet metals with soft solder. There are many kinds of flux for silver soldering. Some are better than others. The most commonly used flux is plain borax and water. Place a lump of prepared borax, purchased from a supply house, in a glass of clear, cold water for about ten minutes before using. Borax is a mineral and will not dissolve in water, but a thick or thin solution of it suspended in the water will do the trick. Flux is used to prevent the silver from oxidizing, as silver solder will not adhere to

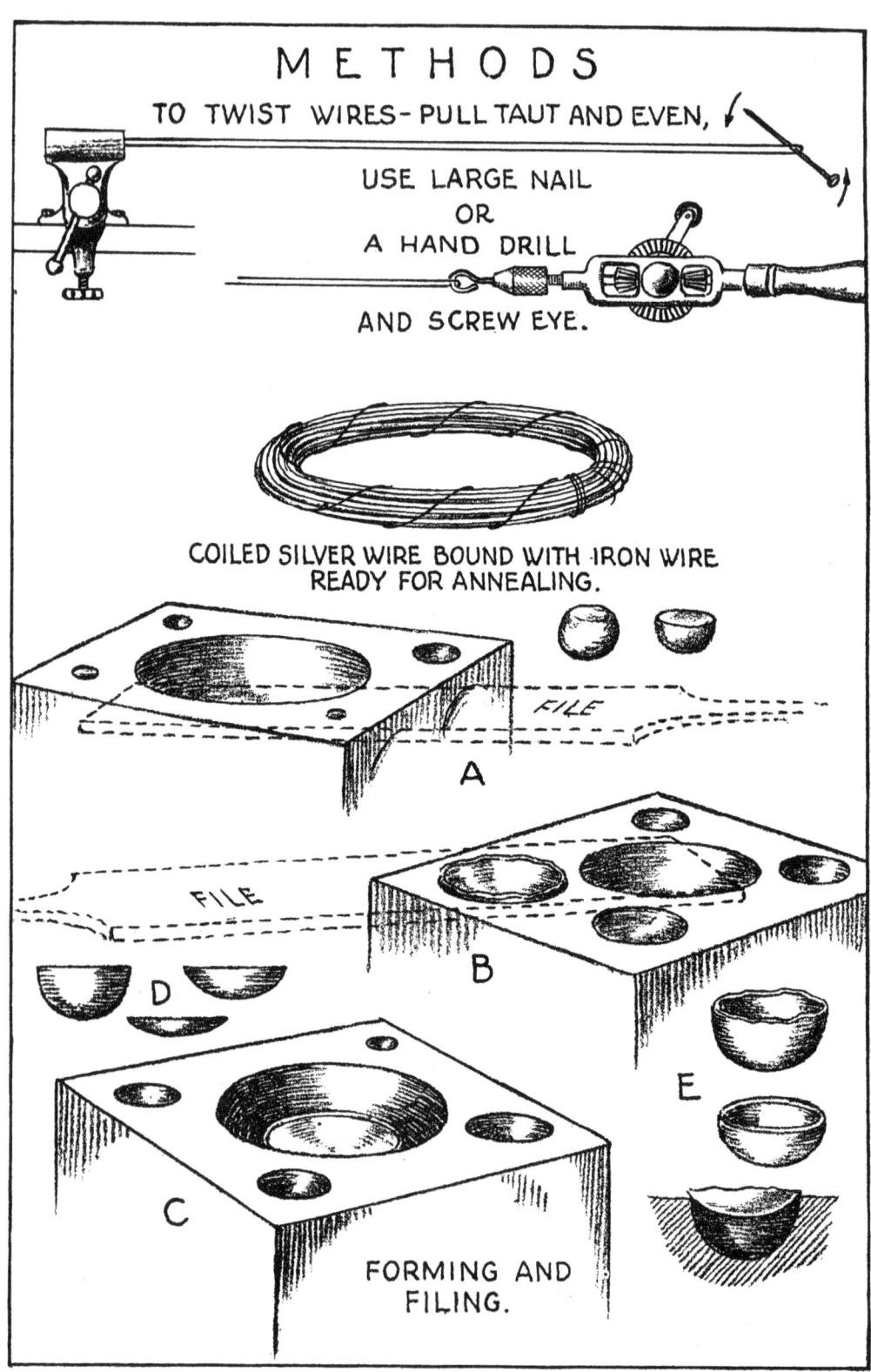

PLATE 5

any oxidized surface, regardless of how much heat is applied. Neither will solder adhere to greasy surfaces. The joint must be absolutely clean.

Easy solder is fluid at 1325 deg. F.
Medium solder is fluid at 1390 deg. F.
Borax is fluid at 1400 deg. F.
Hard solder is fluid at 1425 deg. F.
Sterling silver is fluid at 1640 deg. F.

A beginner should try out the different solders and fluxes before actually doing any soldering on a project. That will acquaint him with the action of the flux, the solder, and the silver. It is quite discouraging to have the silver cut, filed, and fitted nicely, and then spoil the whole job in the last operation, namely, the soldering.

Before trying to solder, make a few *raindrops* to see how easily sterling silver melts. Take a piece of 20-ga. silver about ⅛ in. square, place it on a charcoal block, put a drop of flux on it, and apply the flame. It will quickly become red, then melt and roll up into a small ball. Let it cool a bit, pick it up with a pair of tweezers (copper preferred), and drop it into a small dish of pickle, consisting of ¼ sulphuric acid to ¾ water. (*When mixing the acid and the water, be sure to pour the acid very slowly into the water. If water is poured into the acid, serious burns may be the result.*) This little piece of silver will be white and round with a slightly flattened base. It does not require a great amount of heat to melt the silver. Many of these raindrops will be needed later to decorate Indian jewelry, so save all that are made for future use.

FIG. 2. Silver soldering equipment

The first soldering should be done with any easy-flowing solder and borax. Place either stick or powdered borax, as used in kitchens, into a depression in a borax slab made of slate. Place a few drops of water into the slab depression, and rub the borax stick around until a paste has been formed. When powdered borax is used, simply mix it with water, using a camel's-hair quill brush.

Place a piece of silver about 1 by 1½ in. on a charcoal block and, with the brush, place a drop of flux on the middle of it. Work the flux around, and if it creeps, the silver is not clean and may be a bit greasy. Clean the silver by rubbing it with powdered pumice or crocus cloth. Then try again. If you have done a good job of cleaning, the flux will stay where it is put. Now place a ½- by ¼-in. piece of silver on edge across the larger piece of silver. File the smaller piece so that it stands at right angles to the base piece. Apply flux to the bottom edge and up the sides for 1/16 in. or so. Now cut two small snippets of silver solder, place them in the flux on the slab to coat them with the flux, and lay them at the joint. Gradually apply heat. If the solder suddenly jumps away from the joint, the metal is being heated too fast, thus forming steam which throws the solder out of place.

The larger pieces, in all soldering operations, must be given the same amount of heat as the smaller pieces. This can be done by heating gradually, moving the flame at all times. If the heat is applied too fast, the solder will melt and ball up. When done correctly, the water evaporates slowly, the silver becomes red hot, and then the solder melts and flows along the joint. You cannot see the flux melt; it bubbles up first and then seems to dry out. When that takes place, watch carefully, and apply the flame over both pieces until the solder melts and flows along the joint. Solder also *follows the heat*. The entire soldering operation is rather delicate but interesting, and with a little experimenting and practice it can be done skillfully and correctly.

The method just described shows soldering in its simplest form, and with practice will come assurance. Soldering will seem difficult at times, but experience will tell how and when the solder will flow. Remember not to let the flame play on one part of the work too long. There will be times when heat must be applied to the bottom as well as the top of the work. It is soldering that makes a silversmith proficient, for no matter how well the silver has been designed, filed, shaped, and fitted, if the parts are not successfully soldered, the completed silver piece never will be satisfactory.

There must be plenty of heat while soldering with the use of a blowtorch, a gas flame, or a Prestolite flame. Experiment with the flame also. It should not *blow*. An even blue flame works best, but there should be enough of it to thoroughly heat the work. Indian silversmiths use their gasoline blowtorches to solder the smallest earrings and finger rings as well as the large bracelets and bow guards. It is just knowing how, and that takes practice. The first four or five years, the author used a large plumber's blowtorch for all soldering while doing Indian silversmithing. It is still in his shop to use in case of a gas shortage while in the midst of work, and is shown in Figure 2.

Silver

In addition to the tools required for silversmithing, the silver itself is necessary. The old-time Indian liked Mexican coin silver. The old pesos that the Indians melted for their jewelry probably were of a good grade of silver. The pesos issued for some years previous and until about 1940 were 0.720 fine and could be used for jewelry. These pesos were $1\frac{5}{16}$ in. in diameter. Then about 1947 two new coins were struck, a one-peso piece and a five-peso piece. The one peso is 0.500 fine and $1\frac{1}{4}$ in. in diameter. The five peso is of a good quality of silver, marked 0.900. However, coin silver in sheet form can be obtained from some firms, but sterling silver is stocked wherever jewelers' supplies are sold. Pure silver is too soft for ordinary jewelry work except for bezels. Sterling silver is an alloy of 925 parts pure silver and 75 parts copper, and is known as 925–1000 fine. Sterling silver comes in sheet and wire form. Sterling can be had in thicknesses of 14, 16, 18, 20, 22, 24, and 26 Brown & Sharpe gauge, the smallest number being the thickest metal.

For ordinary work, it is well to buy some 16-, 18-, and 20-ga. silver perhaps 6 in. wide by whatever length is required. The 6-in. width is suggested because that is the usual length for a bracelet, and that is about the longest piece of silver that will be used for making Indian jewelry. Twenty-gauge silver is just about $\frac{1}{32}$ in. thick, while 16 ga. is about $\frac{3}{64}$ in. thick. A piece of 26-ga. silver should be bought for making bezels. Bezels are the little rims soldered to jewelry to hold turquoise or other stones. B. & S. 26-ga. silver is about $\frac{1}{64}$ in. thick. Silver usually is sold by weight, but in ordering, it is customary to state the gauge and the dimensions desired.

Silver wire also should be on hand. This comes in thicknesses ranging from 14 to 30 B. & S. gauge. If a drawplate is among the equipment, the buying of wire is greatly simplified as one gauge of wire is all that is necessary because the smaller sizes can be drawn as needed. In that case, order only 14 or 16 B. & S. gauge wire.

With no drawplate on hand a few feet of 22 and 24 B. & S. gauge wire also will be needed.

It is always easier to work with annealed silver. Silver wire usually comes annealed, but it is sometimes necessary to anneal sheet silver. Hammering silver tends to harden it, and drawing wire through a drawplate also tends to harden it. For this reason, wire usually is pulled through two holes and then coiled, heated, and immersed in cold water or a pickle solution before drawing it thinner or shaping it.

Three more items of equipment will be needed before beginning work. Stone or glass jars for water and the pickle bath are important. Two one-gallon stone crocks are ideal where only one or two persons are working, one for clean water and one for the pickle. Another item is a small pyrex frying pan 7 in. in diameter. This can be set on a small electrical heating unit or on a gas flame whenever anything is to be heated. After a silver piece has been finished, it is placed in this pyrex dish with enough pickle to cover it, and by heating the pickle, the silver becomes snow white. It is then taken out with a wood or copper tweezers, rinsed in clear water with a little baking soda added, and dried. It is now ready to be polished. While it is not considered good practice to get one's hands in the rinse water, it frequently does happen. Because sulphuric acid is hard on the hands, a little baking soda is added to the rinse water to help counteract the sulphuric acid of the pickle bath that is washed off the silver.

Concha Buttons

THE easiest thing to make of silver is a button. Therefore, buttons will be a good project to begin with. Concha buttons are made in all sizes, with quite a variety of designs and with only one simple soldering operation, that of soldering the loop to the back. Concha buttons often are small replicas of the larger conchas made for belts. Sizes, of course, are governed by their use, so, although the drawings are all about 1 in., the buttons may be made smaller or larger to suit their purpose.

Do not use a compass to inscribe the circle as it leaves a telltale center

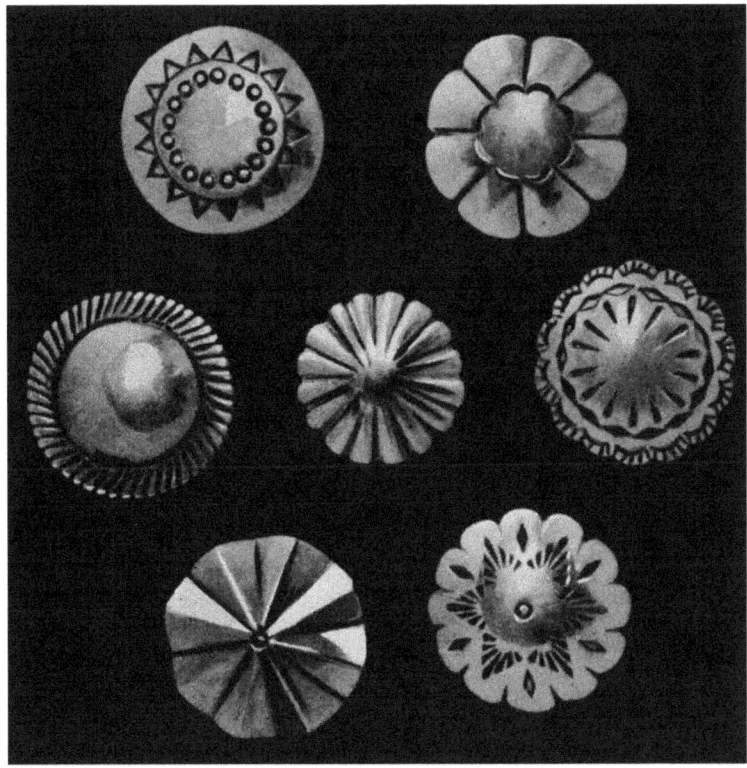

FIG. 3.   Buttons made by the author

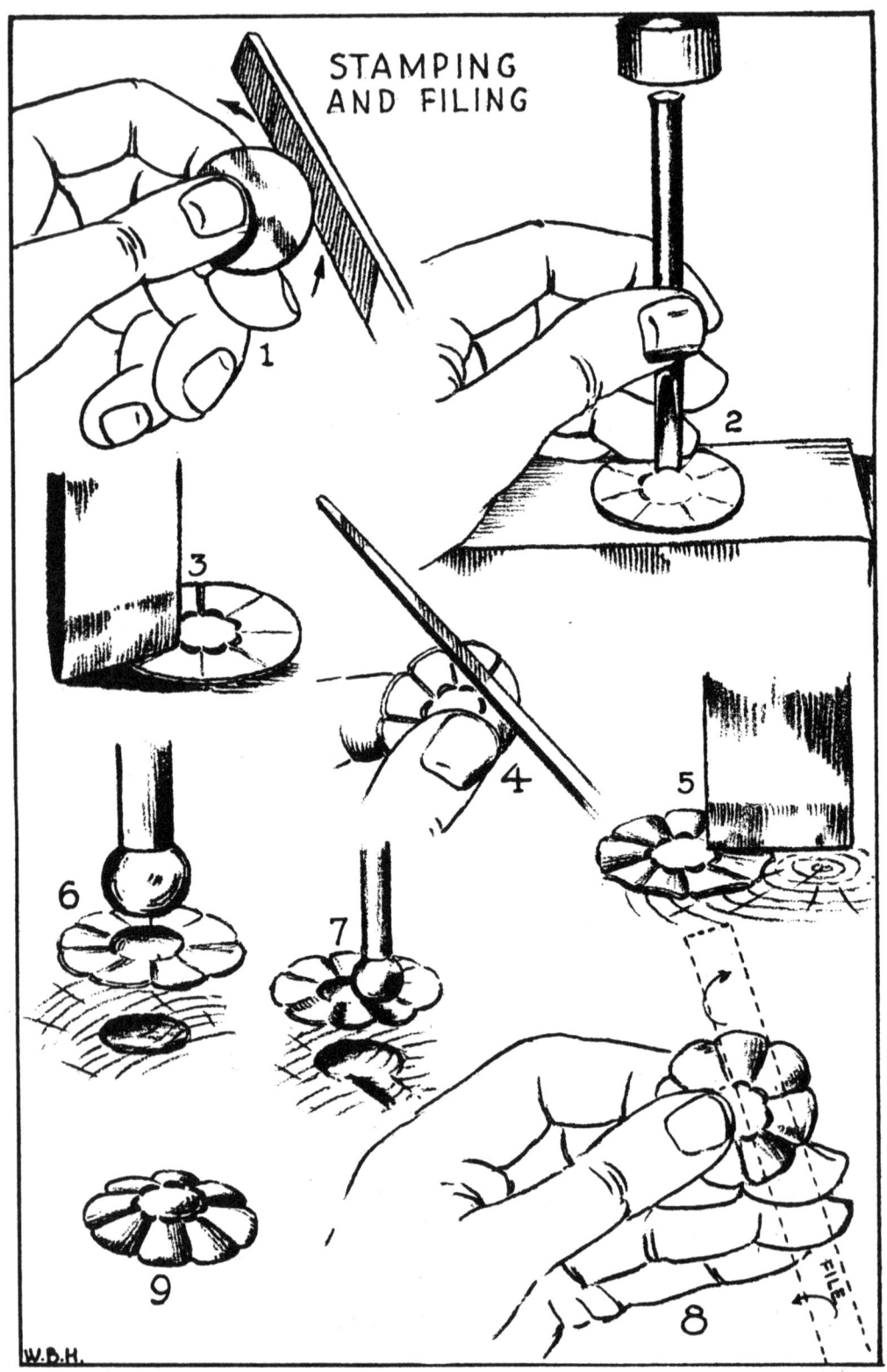

PLATE 6

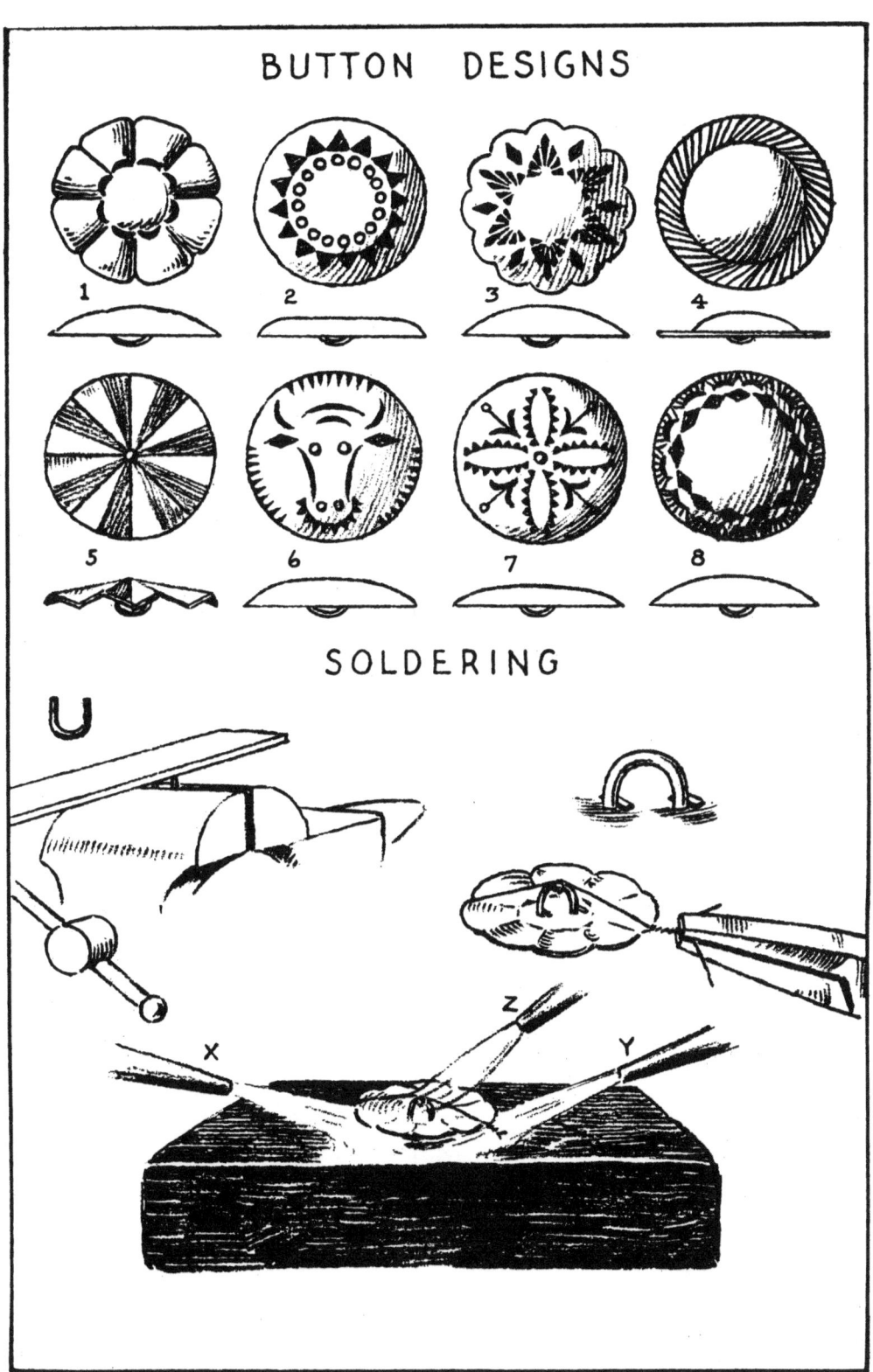

mark which spoils the button's appearance. Instead, use a cardboard template or any round object such as a coin or another button, and mark around it onto the silver. Twenty-gauge silver is ideal for buttons. After laying out the desired number of disks on a piece of silver, cut them out with either a small tin snips or a jeweler's saw. Working with tin snips is much quicker. True up the edges of the disks with a file as shown in 1, Plate 6. For the first button, make 1, Plate 7. Lay on a smaller circle, and quarter the outer area. Then bisect the quarters. Take a small moon-shaped die, and stamp around the smaller circle and between the radial lines as shown in 2, Plate 6. Notice how the third finger of the left hand holds down the disk. These first stampings should be done on the anvil. Now, with a straight die, stamp the radial lines, as shown in 3, Plate 6. If the disk twists slightly out of shape, turn it face down on a block of wood and hammer it flat again. File the petals with a small triangular or square file, as shown in 4, Plate 6. It is well to hold the disk as shown, rather than in a vise, thus avoiding vise marks, and, then too, the work can be held over the filing drawer to save all the filings. Lay the disk face up on a block of wood and hammer the lines down still more. The petals now begin to assume a rounded shape as shown in 5, Plate 6. Next, make a shallow depression in the end grain of the wood block with a round stamp. Then turn the disk face down and bump down the center

FIG. 4.   Modern Navaho buttons in old patterns
(Courtesy The Taylor Museum, Colorado Springs, Colo.)

slightly as shown in 6, Plate 6. Shape the petals as shown in 7, Plate 6. Note how the block is shaped. When the disk has taken on the shape shown in 9, Plate 6, it is ready for filing. Illustration 8, Plate 6, shows how the file is used. This takes care of all irregularities due to hammering. The finer the file, the less polishing must be done later on. Finish up with crocus cloth to take out most of the file marks, or use an emery bob.

Before polishing, solder the loop to the back of the button. Bend a small U shape, cut it off, and file the ends square, as shown in Plate 7. Sometimes these loops can be set in place and soldered, but as a rule they must be held in some way. For the best results, wire the loop in place, using thin, black, annealed iron wire. Scrape or sand the place where the loop is to be attached, wire the loop in position, and place flux and two small snippets of solder at the two ends. Place the button on a charcoal block, and slowly apply heat evenly, below and above as shown at X, Y, and Z, Plate 7, until the solder flows. Then, polish the button. The loops should be high enough to allow a needle to pass through.

The button in 2, Plate 7, is made with a triangular stamp and a small nail set. The edges of the disk are rounded from the back on a block of wood. The button in 3, Plate 5, is stamped first and domed in a large dapping-block depression or on a wood block. In 4, Plate 7, the button has a large circle outlined with a suitable die, and the edge design is made with a small straight die. The center only is domed. The one in 5, Plate 7, is made entirely with the wide straight die shown in 3, Plate 6, with a small nail-set mark for the center. Stamp from the front first on the anvil. Turn it over and stamp the back, also on the anvil. Then use the wood block, hammering first from the back and then from the front with the same large die. The buttons in 6, 7, and 8, Plate 7, are punched with different dies. The doming is done after the designs have been punched.

After doming, take a clean flat file and go over the entire surface, holding the disks as in 8, Plate 6. This produces an even surface. Filing also takes down the small ridges of silver that the die punches press up around each stamping.

After the filing has been done, solder on the loop and polish the button.

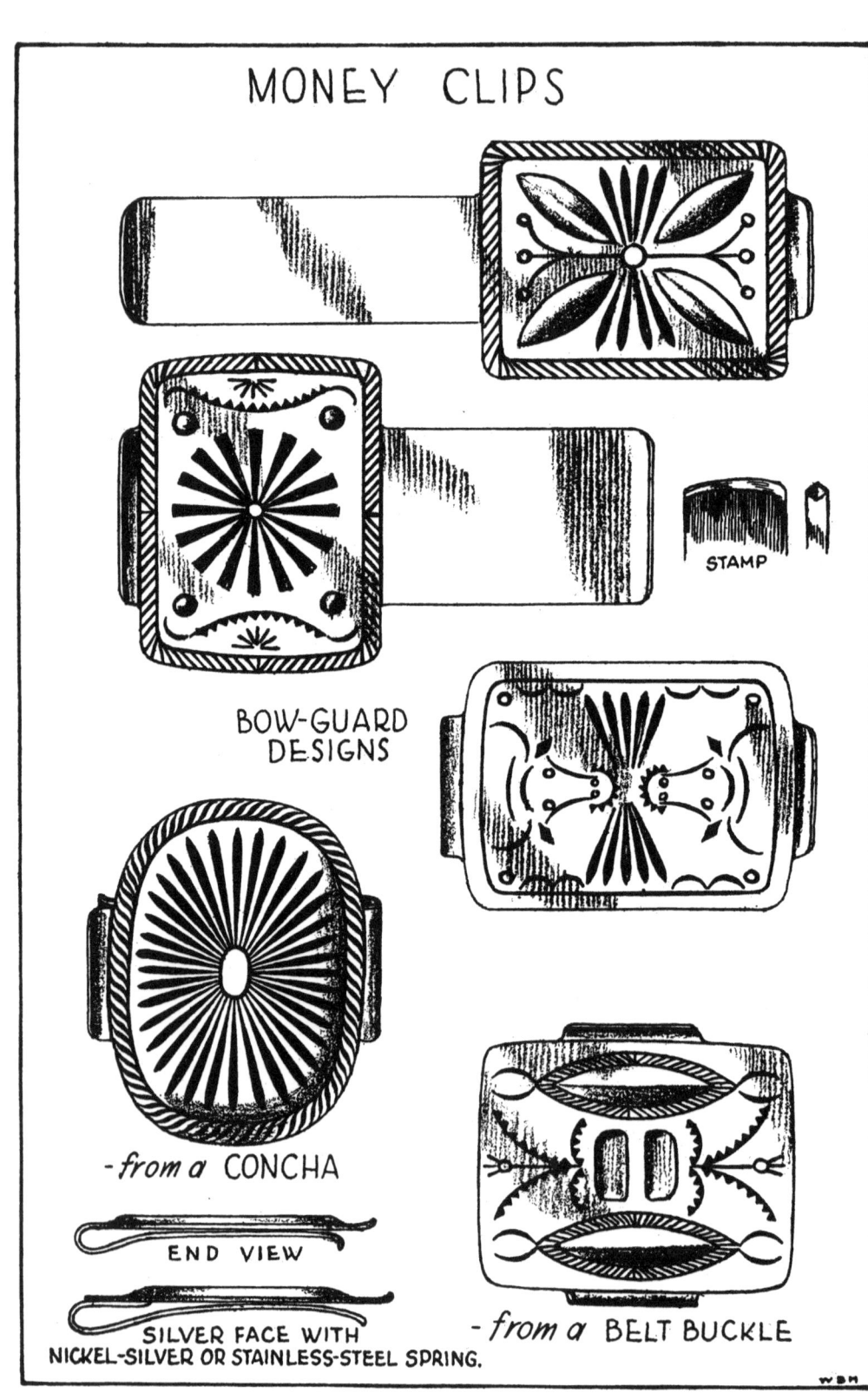

Money Clips

THE money clip is a new innovation in Indian silversmithing. The Indian has no special design for this modern new article, but he uses the same designs as on his bow guards, buckles, and conchas.

One drawback in making the clips and tie clasps is that silver must be heated to make the springs, and the heating causes the silver to become soft.

There are two ways to overcome that difficulty. One is to use nickel silver and the other is to solder a clasp of nickel silver or stainless steel to the face of the clip. The clip at the top of Plate 8 has a spring soldered to it, while the one with the cows' heads is made of one piece of nickel silver. The tie clasps and hair clips in Plate 9 are made of nickel silver, and the bezels are of sterling silver. Soldering is done as when working sterling silver. Metal can be 20 ga. or even a little thinner.

It is well to make the stamp shown in Plate 8 to use in decorating these clips. Be sure the angle of the stamp is blunt, which makes stamping easier. For the stampings on the money clips use a straight liner first, and then, with this new stamp, follow the groove and widen it. The raised parts of the upper money clip in Plate 8 are bumped up from the back on the end of a log, as shown in 7, Plate 6. Money clips are made without turquoise, because the stones would soon become scratched if the clip and other coins were kept in the same pocket.

FIG. 5. Money clips

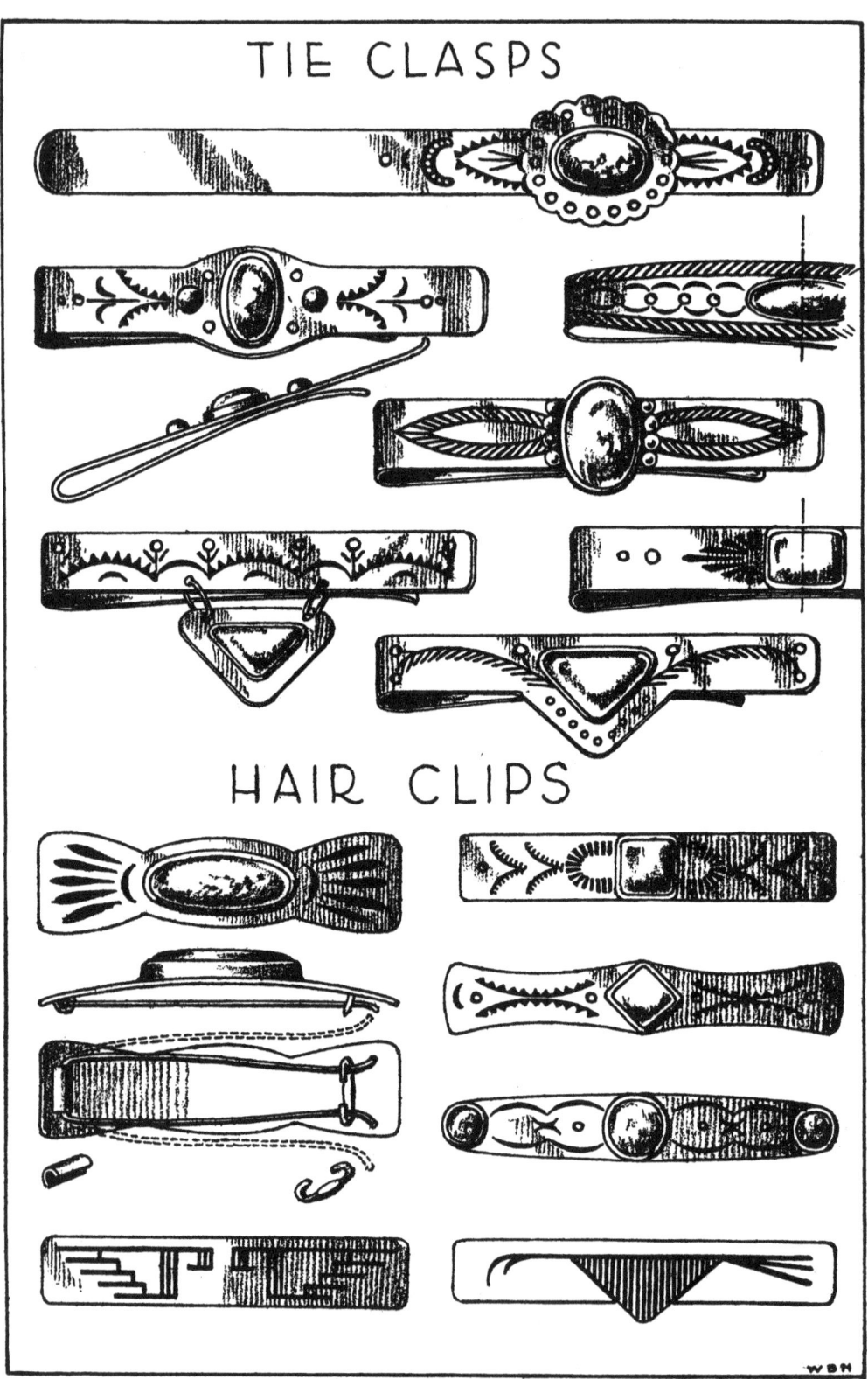

Tie Clasps and Hair Clips

TIE clasps, like money clips, require a fairly good spring. Therefore, it is suggested that nickel silver be used. The clasps shown on Plate 9 were made of 24-ga. B. & S.

Hair clips may be made of silver, including the wire, which can be stiffened by drawing it through a drawplate. It is advisable to buy a few feet of 10-ga. wire which can be drawn down to any size. The wire on the hair clips is drawn down to 16 ga., and if pulled through the last two holes without annealing, will be springy enough and yet remain pliable so that it can be bent to the required shape.

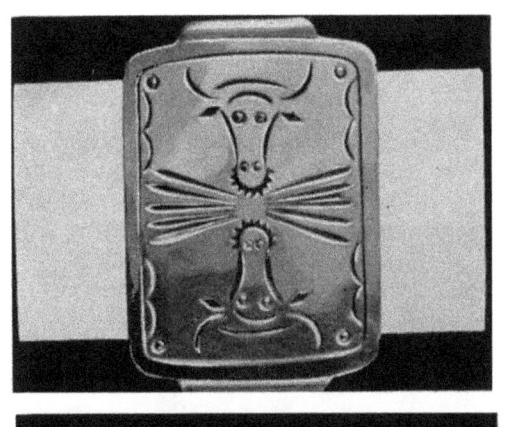

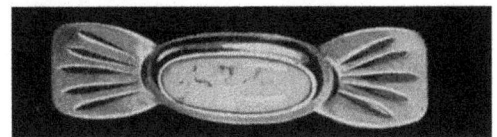

FIG. 6. Money clips, tie clasps, and hair clips

Lapel Pins and Brooches

THE lapel pins in Plate 10 are popular items in the southwest trading posts. The bird designs, taken from old Pueblo pottery, seem very appropriate for the pins. Designs of this kind may be found in ethnology books for the most part, but they also may be found in books on Pueblo pottery.

No special tools are required to make these pins, because the punches used are the same as those which made the designs and stampings in Plate 4.

Twenty-gauge B. & S. silver is ideal for these pins. The best and easiest way to cut out the pins, after they have been traced or drawn on the metal, is with a jeweler's saw. The cutting stroke of the saw is downward as shown in the upper left-hand sketch in Plate 11. Keep the saw perpendicular and hold the metal firmly down on the bench pin, cutting right up to the outline. On all the birds' feet, notice that the toe from one foot touches the other foot. This has been done to strengthen the legs which are rather thin. One leg alone would be likely to bend if caught on something.

FIG. 7. Pins embodying old Pueblo designs

For the benefit of those who have never sawed fine jewelry, first drill a small hole between the bird's legs, insert one end of the saw blade through the hole, and fasten the saw blade in the frame. Now cut out the section, then loosen one end of the saw blade, and remove the blade. Jewelers' saw blades always should be unclamped on one end to take the tension off the frame when the saw is not in use.

When no jeweler's saw is handy, the larger parts can be cut out with a small tin snips, and the smaller parts with a small cold chisel. Do not cut on the surface of the anvil, which would spoil the face of the anvil with chisel cuts. Use some other flat piece of iron. Chisel-cut objects naturally call for quite a bit of filing, but that is the old Indian way of cutting and shaping silver. The saw-cut brooches also must be filed smooth along the outer edges, as sawing causes burrs to form on the edges.

After the blanks have been cut and filed, stamp the ornaments on them. The illustration in the lower left-hand corner of Plate 11 shows how to make the large round die used to stamp the eyes of the upper two lapel pins in Plate 10. A piece of annealed drill rod or other steel rod is center punched and drilled. The edge can be trued up with a file if the drilling is not exactly in the center of the rod.

To dome the lapel pins, lay them on the log end and carefully hammer from the back. Use the ball end of a ball-peen hammer and be careful not to have a lot of small bumps instead of one large one. The Shumopovi pin in Plate 10 is left flat but the one below to the left of it can be domed on a dapping block. The sun-god symbol is flat except for the center circle.

The two lower bird pins in Plate 10 look as if they were cut out of rather large pieces of silver. This is not necessary because these pins can be made out of pieces of silver obtained from the scrap box. The wings, the bodies, the head, and the feathers may all be cut out of separate pieces of scrap silver. They are cut to shape first and then laid on a charcoal block, soldered, and filed smooth. Many small pieces, that ordinarily would be melted over and rolled into sheets, can be used for soldering them together.

The fasteners or pins now must be attached. Number 1, Plate 11, shows the conventional type of pin which is bought in three parts, pin, joint, and catch. The rivet is merely a piece of wire cut to the proper length. To solder this assembly, proceed as shown in the lower left-hand corner of Plate 11. The pin is left off until after the soldering so as not to heat and anneal or soften it. A piece of iron wire running through the joint and catch, as shown, will keep those two parts in correct position for soldering. Apply the flux, place a small piece of solder beside each part, and then apply the heat. After the pieces have been soldered, remove the iron wire and place the silver pin in the pickle jar to remove the flux and to whiten or clean the metal. There are two ways of using the

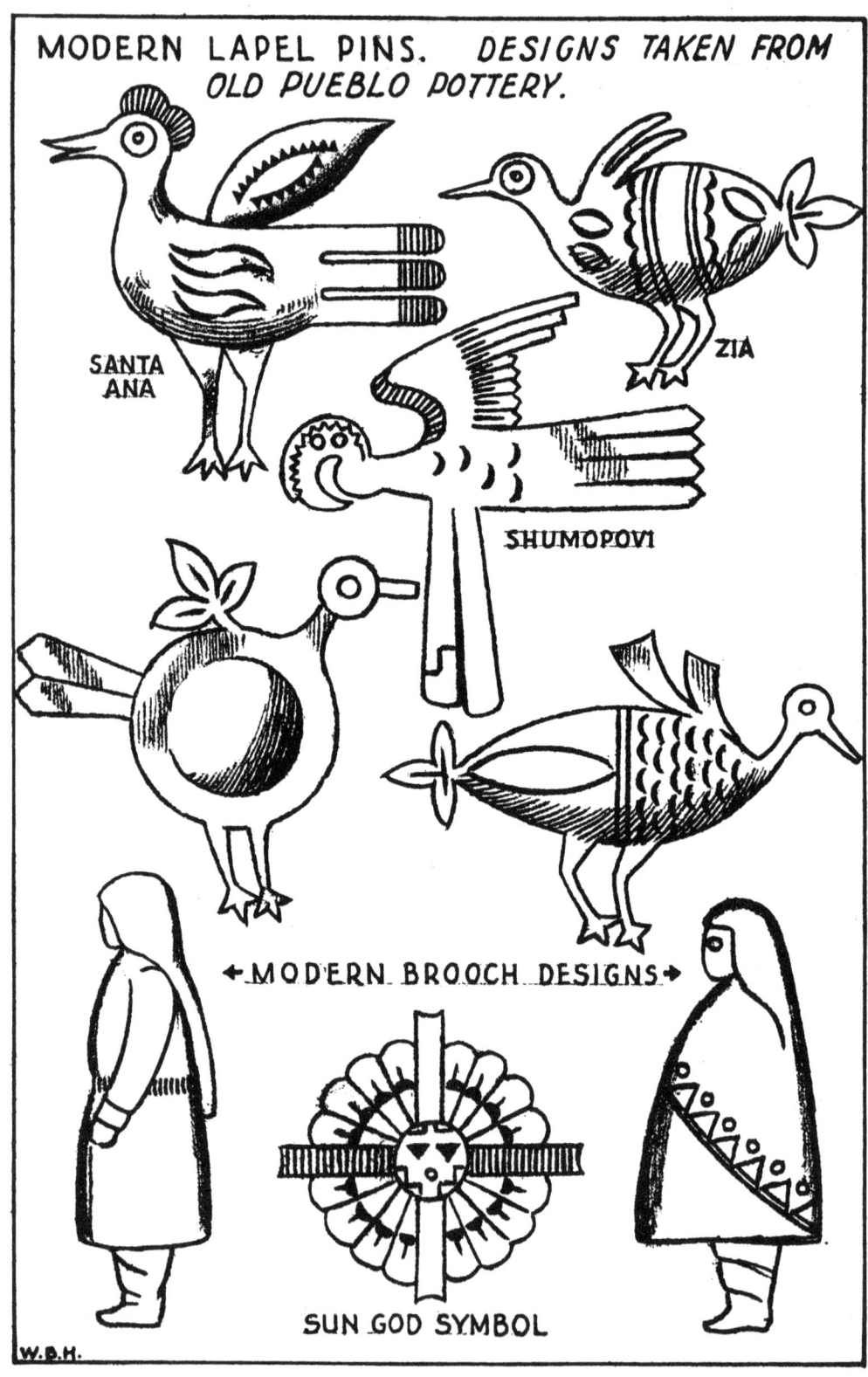

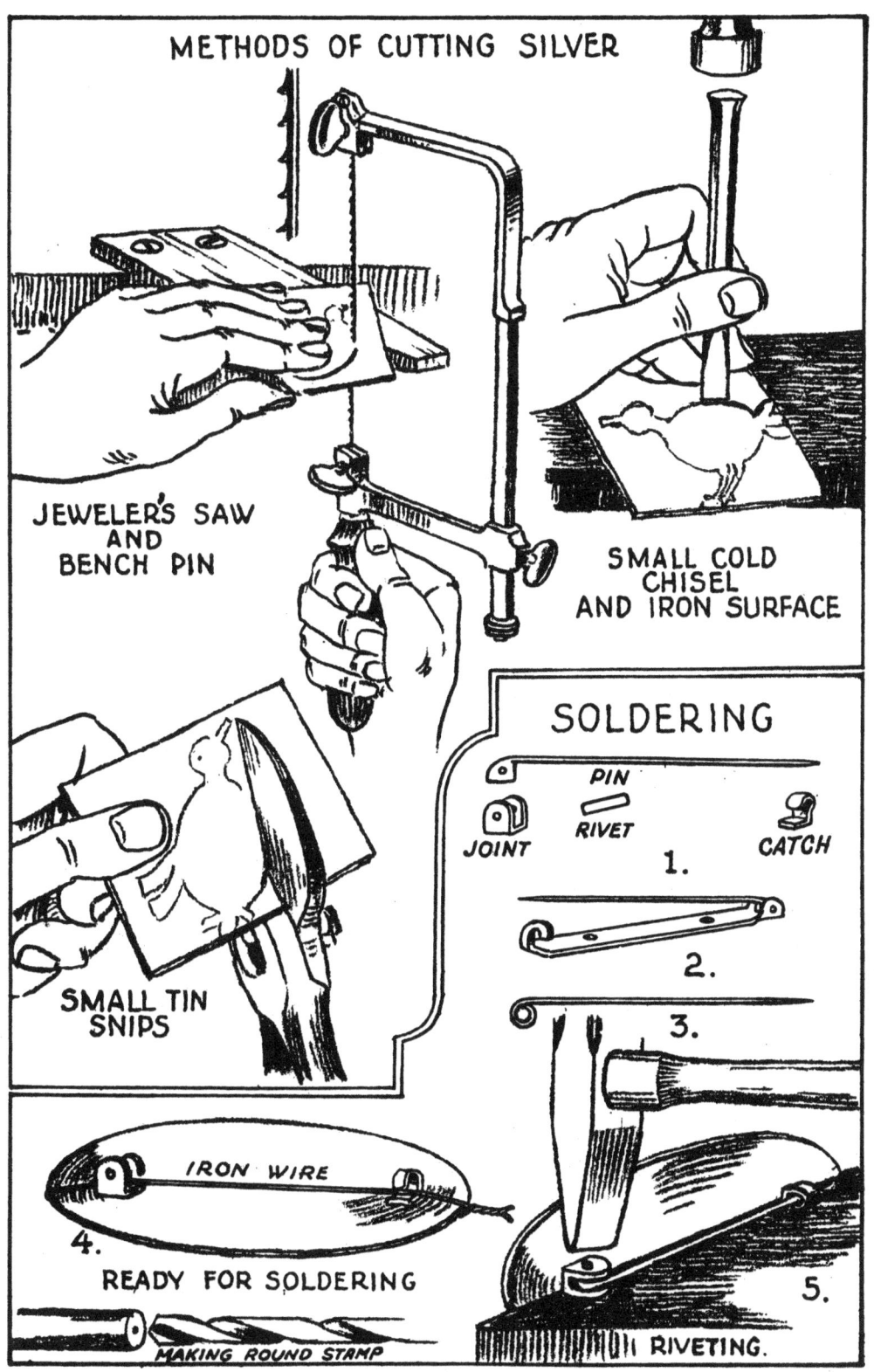

pickle, which consists of ¼ sulphuric acid and ¾ water. The metal can be heated and dropped into the pickle, or the metal can be placed in the pyrex pan, covered with pickle, and the pan set over a flame until the metal becomes white. If the iron wire is left on the pin, or if a steel tweezer is used on the silver while it is in the pickle, a reddish or brownish deposit will form on the silver. This is very difficult to buff off. Therefore, use copper tweezers or one made of wood to remove objects from the pickle. When the metal is clean and white, polish it on a buffing wheel if it has been smoothly rounded. If it has not been rounded, smooth it with a file. Then insert the pin and the short piece of wire, and gently rivet the wire by tapping first one side and then the other. Indians sometimes use a piece of wire longer than the joint is wide and bend the wire at right angles on both sides of the joint to hold it in place. The pin shown in 3, Plate 11, also can be made.

Number 2, Plate 11, shows a cheaper fastener used for wooden and plastic jewelry. This type of fastener should be sweated on with 50-50 tinner's solder. Coat the back of the silver pin with soft solder. Then set the fastener in place, and heat the metal from below until the solder melts. Use the same borax flux that is used for hard solder.

Rings Without Settings

A RING is a fine, one-evening project. Even a fairly complicated ring, including the setting of one or more stones, may be finished in that time. Before attempting any complicated work, however, it is well to try a few solid silver rings without settings.

For the first project, try a pair of "friendship rings." They are usually made in pairs, one for the girl and one for the boy friend. First, get the measurements of the fingers which the rings are to fit. Use a ⅛-in. strip of paper to get these measurements, or a ring that fits, or use a ring gauge. Cut strips of 18-ga. silver ⁵⁄₁₆ in. wide and a little longer than is needed (¹⁄₁₆ in. longer is just about right).

Before proceeding, study the design which has been chosen, and see whether the required stamping punches are on hand. If not, they may be

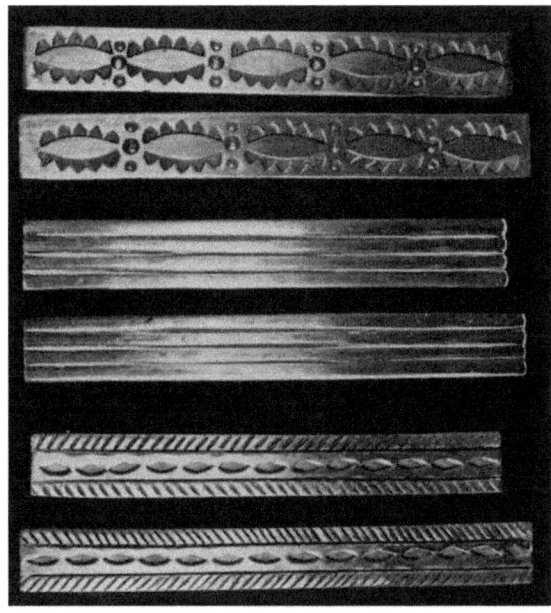

FIG. 8. Ring blanks stamped and ready for soldering

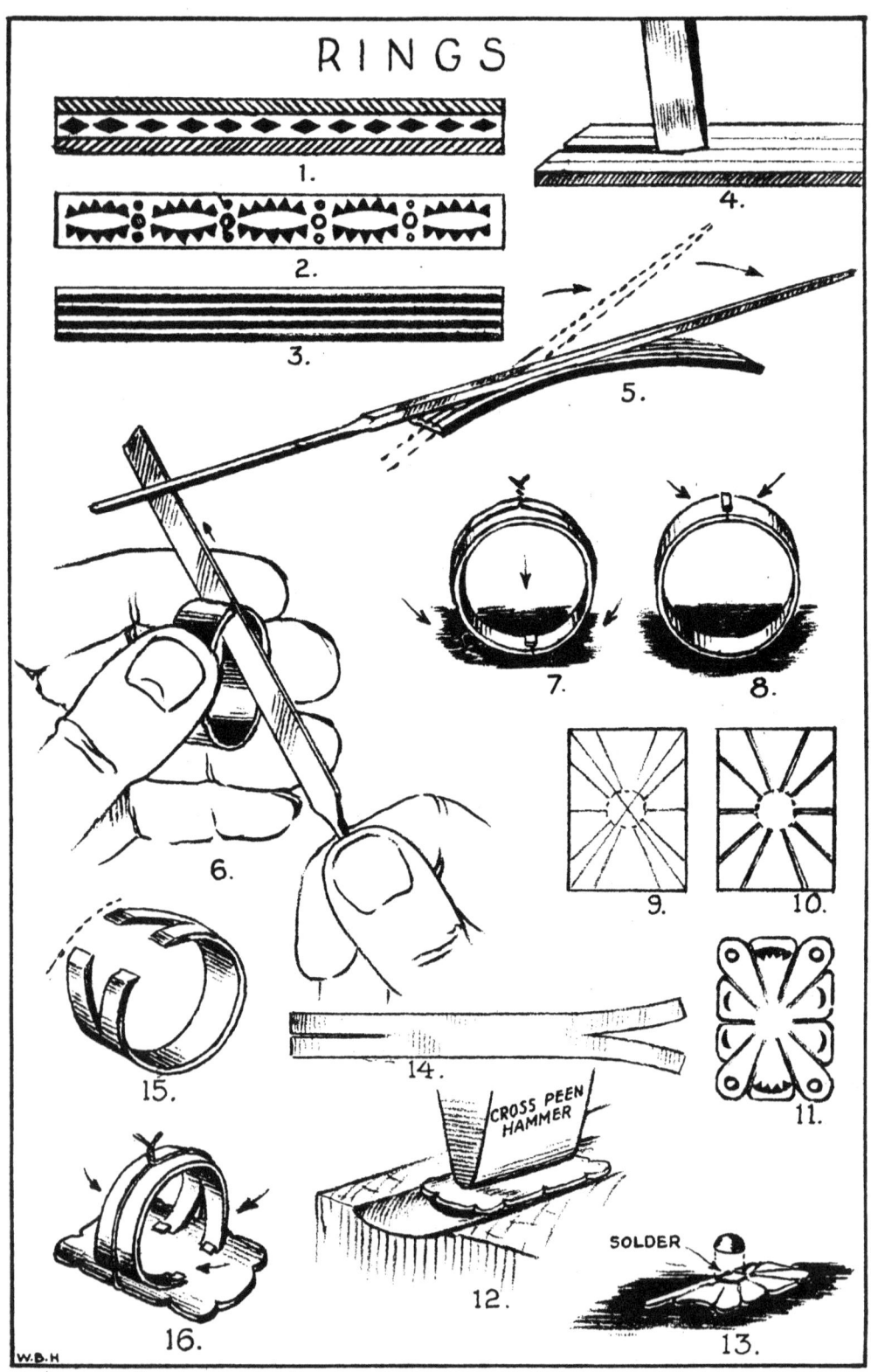

PLATE 12

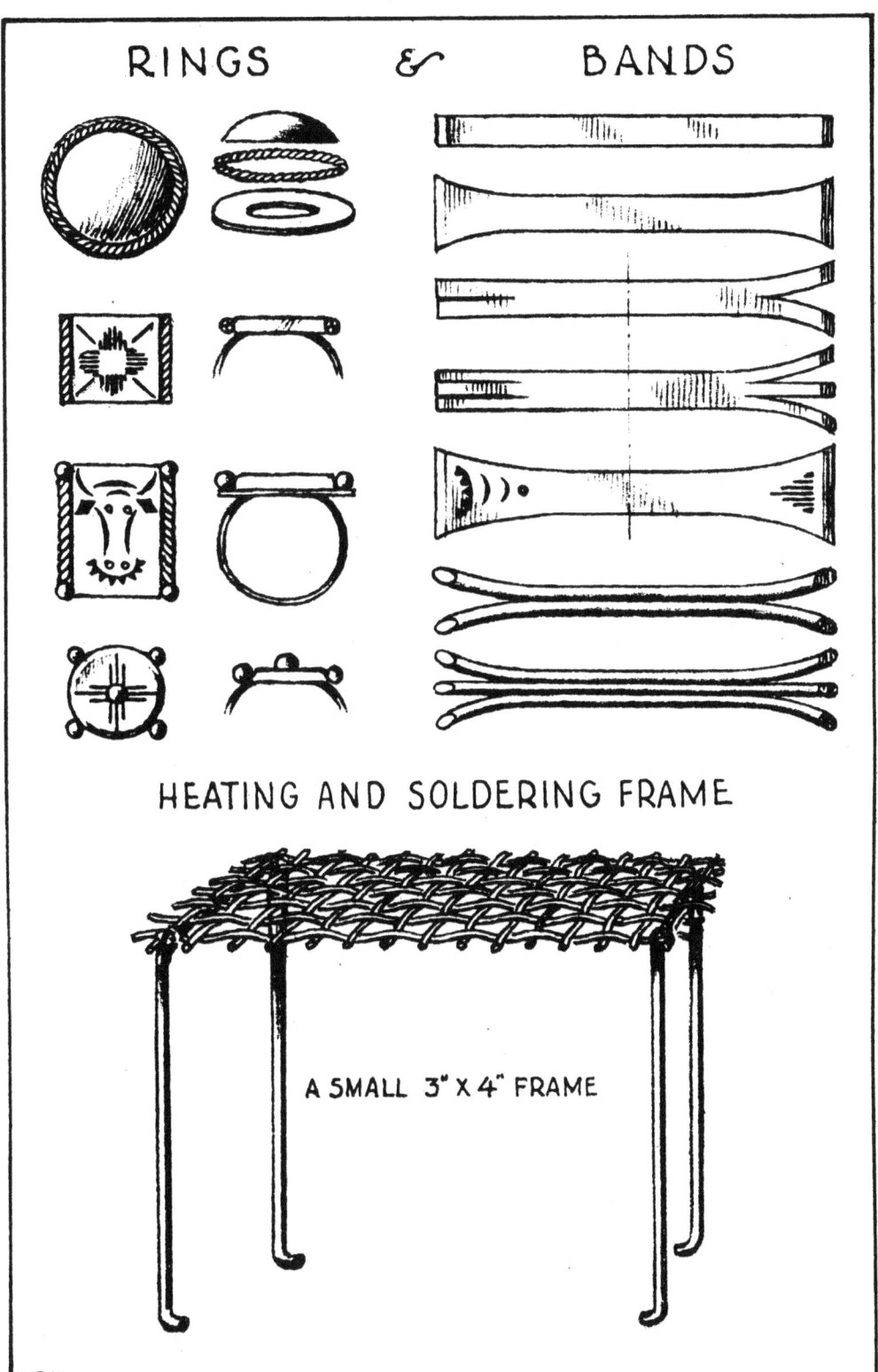

made without much trouble. It is well to keep several sizes of drill rod and some small ten- or fifteen-cent cold chisels on hand, so that, when a new stamping punch is needed, it can be made without unnecessary delay.

The ring band shown in 1, Plate 12, is made with a straight liner and a small diamond stamp. With a pointed scriber, scratch a line $1/16$ or $3/32$ in. from each edge. With the liner and a small hammer, make the two long grooves along the scribed lines, and then stamp in the diagonal lines. These diagonal lines also may be made with a compound curved tool as shown at e, Plate 4. It will be noticed that the edges of the ring band will bulge out where the stamp overlaps them. After the diagonal lines have been punched, round or square off the edges with a file. The diamonds are punched as shown.

The design in Number 2 is made with a curved saw-toothed stamp and two hollow-point nail sets. First, lay the silver blank for the ring on a piece of blotting paper, and trace around the blank with a pencil. Then press the stamp into the blotting paper, and the design will show as it will appear on the silver. Omit the nail-set punches at the ends until after the ring has been soldered. Then place the ring over the horn of the anvil, and put in the three punch marks over the soldered joint.

The blank in Number 3 is made out of stock $5/16$ in. wide. Scribe a line down the center and then two lines centered at each side of it, dividing the width into four equal parts. With the straight edged stamp or chasing tool, carefully follow the three lines. If the chasing tool is set down into the first depression half its length, as shown in Number 4, and then hammered, the line will be much straighter. Go over each line lightly at first, and then go over it once or twice more until the groove is smooth. The same holds true with stamping a curved line except that a smaller chasing tool must be used. Bend the blank slightly with the fingers to the shape shown in Number 5. Then, with a small file, work down the grooves so they look like the end view sketched to the right of Number 3. It will be much easier to file the band after it has been bent than if left flat. It calls for careful filing to get the effect of four pieces of wire soldered together.

After filing the edges and squaring the ends, shape the rings with a small wood or rawhide mallet over a ring mandrel or other round piece of metal or wood. Then try the ring for size. To make a good soldering joint, the edges should butt up quite truly. To get this result, take a thin file, such as a magneto file or the small flat file that comes in sets of needle files, hold the ring as shown in 6, Plate 12, and run the file between the two ends until they fit snugly.

Then tie the ring together with thin, black, annealed iron wire as shown in Number 7. Be sure the ends are clean and put flux between the ends before wiring.

If the band possesses enough spring, the soldering operation may be done without wiring, as shown in Number 8. There must be enough spring in the band, however, to hold the ends tight and even.

FIG. 9.   Friendship rings

Whichever method is used, place the ring on a charcoal block, put a little more flux on the joint, and a small snippet of solder over that. Be sure the solder also has flux on it. Apply a medium flame slowly until the silver turns dark, and then watch for the flux and solder to melt. After the solder has hardened, remove the iron wire, and place the ring in the pickle bath to dissolve any adhering flux. Then rinse the ring in clear water, dry it, and touch up the joint inside and out with a fine file. It may be necessary also to touch up some of the punch marks. If the band shown in Number 2 is being made, the nail-set marks over the soldered joint must be punched after the ring has been soldered.

Next polish the ring on a buffing wheel with crocus compound, or use an old toothbrush dipped in finely powdered pumice and water. In all buffing, the thing to guard against is not to polish off too much of the stamped design. The file marks should be polished out, but silver is soft, and it does not take much to buff away shallow stamping. The Indians usually stamp their designs quite deep, and these designs are not so easily spoiled by buffing.

The ring in Number 11 is an Indian design, except that it has a *raindrop* soldered to the center instead of a turquoise. This design can be used by anyone who has no stones on hand or none of the right size. It is an attractive ring. To make one like it, cut a piece of 18-ga. silver $1\frac{1}{16}$ by

Modern   Indian   Indian

FIG. 10.   Variety in design

1 in., and lay it out as in Number 9. With a wide, straight-edged chasing tool (a good size is one with a 1-in. cutting edge), stamp the radial lines shown in Number 10, about halfway through the metal. File the edges as shown in Number 11, and stamp the designs. Then curve the blank about halfway between straight and the curve of the ring band. Number 12 shows how this is done on a block of hardwood. Smooth the face with a fine flat file, and then polish before the *raindrop* is soldered to it. To make a large raindrop, take a piece of scrap silver 18 ga. by $3/16$ by $3/8$ in. Lay it on the charcoal block, put flux on it, and heat until it melts and forms a ball. File the flat bottom of the ball by rubbing it on a flat file. Then slightly file the part it is to occupy, for a better fit. Place flux and a piece of thin solder $1/8$ in. square in the center of the ring top, and put the silver ball on it, as shown in Number 13. Let the flux dry, so there will be no chance of steam forming and pushing the ball out of place. Heat the solder evenly and slowly, and when it melts, the ball will settle down in place with a fillet of silver all around the base of it. Occasionally these raindrops slide to one side. To avoid this, heat the entire piece from below, using the soldering frame shown in Plate 13. When the solder melts, push the ball carefully over to where it belongs, with a piece of iron wire.

Next, choose the band that is to be used with this ring. Whether the type of band is like the one in 14, Plate 12, or any one in Plate 13, cut and bend it to shape. Then file the ends as shown in 15, Plate 12, to fit the bottom of the top piece.

When two or more soldering operations follow each other, it is customary to use a hard solder for the first and an easy-flowing solder for the next. For beginners, the use of hard and medium silver solders is a little difficult because their melting points are higher than that of easy-flowing solder and, therefore, nearer to the melting point of sterling silver. It is well, therefore, to postpone the two solder methods and use only easy-flowing solder for the present. To do this, give the first soldered joint a liberal coating of powdered jeweler's rouge and water. Jeweler's rouge is a dark red powder which mixes with water. Mix it to a paste, apply it with a small brush, and let it dry. Its object is to absorb some of the heat. Now put flux on the places where the band touches the plate and on the ends of the band. Then wire band and plate together as shown in Number 16. Put a small snippet of solder on each place of contact, and add more flux. Observe the greatest cleanliness when soldering. The solder must be as clean as the silver. Solder that has been in a box for a while should be rubbed clean with jeweler's rouge or scraped with a knife to remove any grease or dirt.

Now place the assembled ring in 16, Plate 12, on the soldering frame in Plate 13. If the ball is too large, force the wires of the soldering frame apart to allow the ring to lie flat. Apply the heat and, after the solder flows, let it cool a moment. Cut and remove the iron wire and, while still hot, drop the ring gently into the pickle bath. Wash off the rouge with pumice and water. Inspect the job carefully. Perhaps a few places must be touched up a little with a half-round file, and the ring is ready for polishing.

Tarnishing or Antiquing

THE Indian likes his silver jewelry bright and shiny. The white man likes his with a dark tarnish in the low parts and a high polish on the rest of it. To give it this effect, brush the piece with a solution of liver of sulphur (potassium sulphide). The entire surface will immediately turn dark if it is clean. Then polish as before, and the low places will stay dark. This finish was used on the rings shown in the illustrations.

Heating and Soldering Frames

A frame like the one shown in Plate 13 should be on every workbench. The grid is a 3 by 4-in. or a 5 by 7-in. piece of 14-ga. black iron-wire screen with openings about $\frac{1}{8}$ in. square. Make the stand of heavy wire about 5 in. high, and wire it firmly to the grid with binding wire.

The soldering frame is used when it is necessary to apply heat from below as well as from above, as in the case of the ring shown in 16, Plate 12. It also is used for heating pieces of sheet silver or wire for annealing. When annealing, it is advisable to have a large piece of asbestos below the stand or to set the stand in a 12-in. pan filled with coke. This not only prevents burning the bench top but helps to reflect the heat to the pieces being heated.

Turquoise in Indian Jewelry

WHILE the older pieces of southwest Indian jewelry were made with little or no turquoise, the later and more modern Indian jewelry is set with beautiful, rich blue turquoise. To the Indian jewelry worker, turquoise is almost as necessary as silver. In some Zuni jewelry, silver is merely something to hold the turquoise in place. When he cannot get turquoise, he will take the next best in the line of bluish stones for the jewelry he makes for sale.

Good turquoise is of a beautiful blue color. Poor turquoise is lighter in color, sometimes almost white, and quite soft. The Indian likes the rich blue stone for his own jewelry. The lower grades or lighter colored stones often are oiled; that is, the stones are placed in a bath of hot mineral oil, which brings them somewhat up to the color of the better grade. There is no certain way of telling whether or not a stone in a piece of jewelry is oiled except that, in time, the oil dries out and the stone finally reverts back to its original color.

At times, trading posts and jewelry stores have jewelry set with green turquoise. While some of it looks rather pleasing, the Indians do not care for it. Rather than use poor turquoise, malachite may be used. This is a beautiful, deep bluish green. It is mined near copper deposits, like turquoise, but it cannot be purchased as easily as turquoise.

Chrysocolla, which some say is related to turquoise, also is a very pretty stone. It is translucent, and its colors run from dark blue or green to a milky white.

Dioptase is a deep green Arizona stone, which, no doubt, often is passed off and sold for green turquoise. The same is true of vericite, which is a lighter green. Dioptase is found in Utah. It can be easily mistaken for turquoise by unsuspecting buyers. Dealers frequently represent green turquoise as something very rare, but the southwest Indians seldom wear green turquoise.

The best turquoise today comes from Nevada. It was formerly mined in New Mexico, but only a few mines are still in operation in that state.

The stone still is mined in a primitive manner by breaking it out of rock with a pick or a hammer and chisel.

Some turquoise is found in the form of beautifully clear blue nuggets without any matrix while others contain quite a bit. Some of the most magnificent sets are turquoise matrix as shown by the cut stones in Figure 11. The only piece in this group that is a clear blue is second from the left in the bottom row. In Figures 13 and 14, the large stones contain matrix.

Another important feature in turquoise is hardness. Some pieces are so soft that they can be cut with a knife. That kind of stone is not worth setting in silver. Good turquoise is quite hard, and will not scratch easily with everyday wear. It pays to buy from a reliable dealer, whether he is an Indian trader or runs a jeweler's supply house.

Turquoise may be bought either in the rough or as cut stones. Most Indians now buy ready-cut stones although excellent turquoise workers may be found among the Zunis. Figure 12 shows how rough stones look. Cutting and polishing stones is a fascinating hobby in itself, and there is a lot of satisfaction in being able to say you cut the stone as well as made the mounting. More will be said about cutting later. Whether you intend to do any cutting or not, there are times when it is well to know a little something about the art. Such an occasion arises when a

FIG. 11. Examples of cut stones. The stones marked "C" are chrysocolla. The rest are turquoise. Those at the right are spiderweb turquoise. Those in the upper right-hand corner are matched sets for bracelets

FIG. 12. Rough stones. M — Malachite; C — Chrysocolla; T — Turquoise

FIG. 13. These are modern pieces of Indian jewelry and it is safe to say that they were made by Zuni Indians

(Courtesy — Maisels, Albuquerque, N. M.)

stone cracks while it is being set or when one has become loose and has been lost. It is then necessary to reshape a stone to fit into the bezel. If only a small amount of the stone has to be taken off, it can be done with a piece of carborundum or alundum cloth of about 180 grit, mounted on a stick of thin wood and used like a file. If, however, quite a bit has to be ground off, it can be done on any kind of grindstone. The small amount of polishing required for this sort of job can be done on a felt or muslin buffing wheel charged with tin oxide and water.

Petrified or agatized wood, while not a real competitor of turquoise, is finding much popularity in the west. Colorful pieces of this wood, when cut and polished, are very attractive. Sometimes a number of pieces, similar

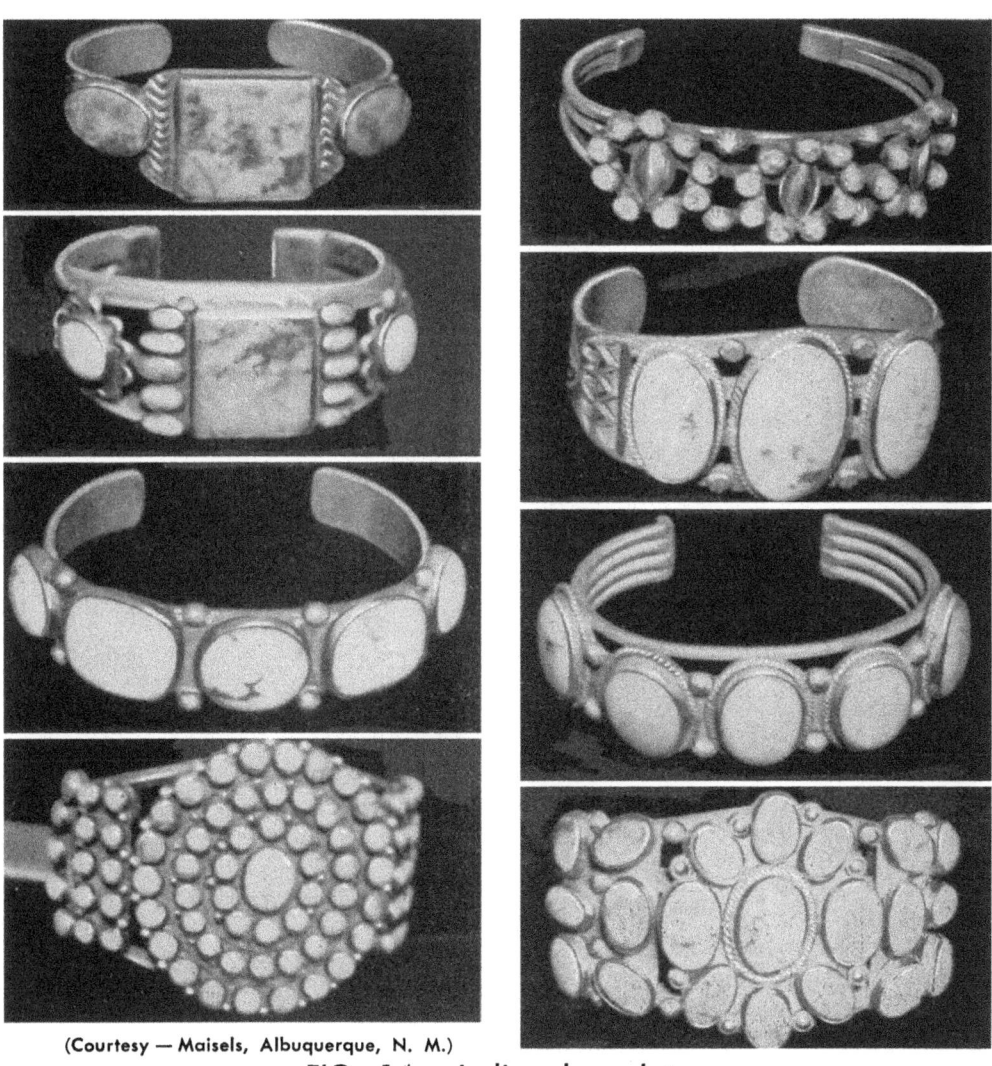

(Courtesy — Maisels, Albuquerque, N. M.)

FIG. 14.   Indian bracelets

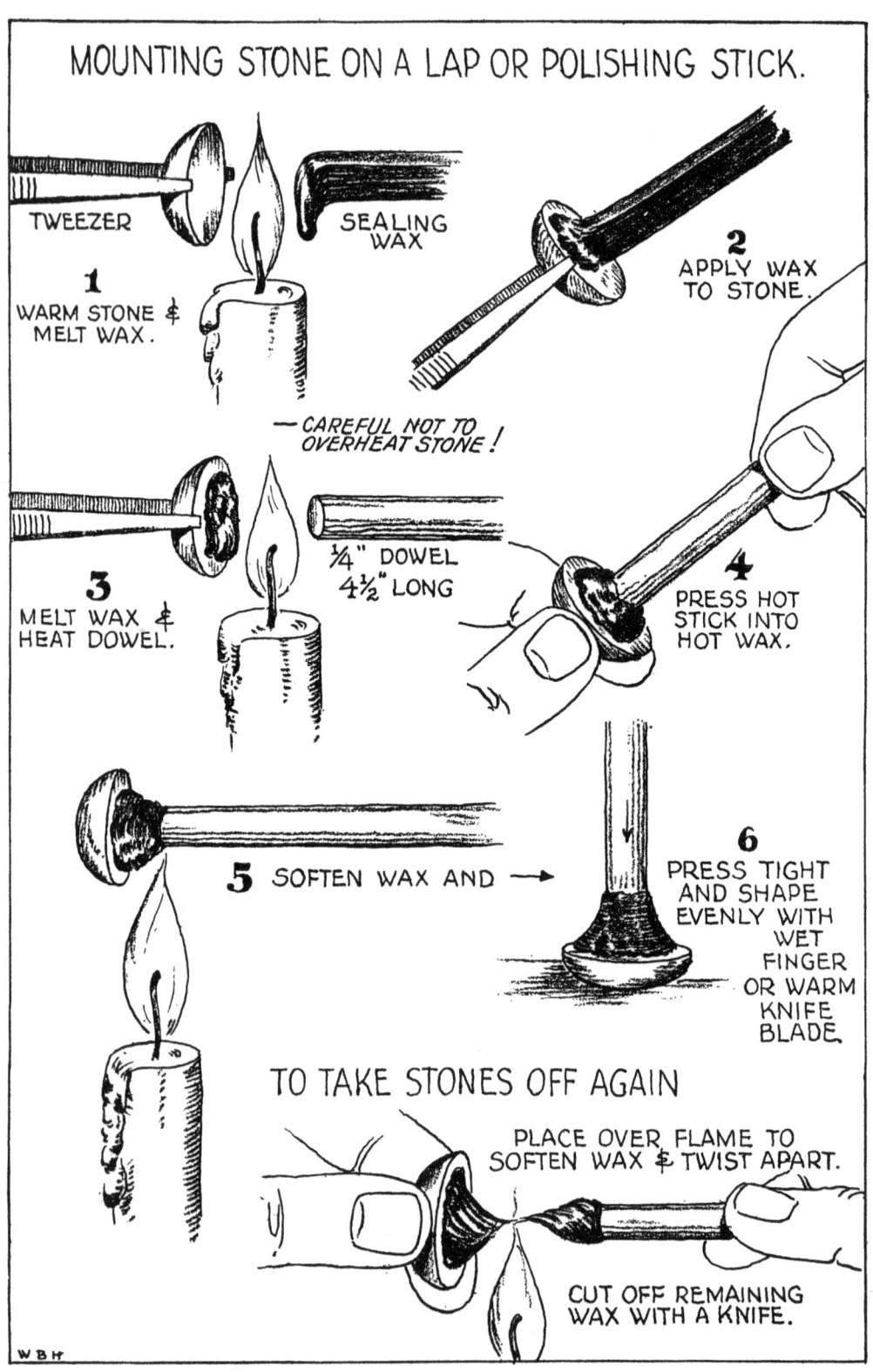

PLATE 14

in color and design, can be cut from one chunk. Such pieces make beautiful matched sets for bracelets, rings, earrings, and pins. Petrified wood is very hard and takes a high polish, but its colors do not show up as in the turquoise. To be truly appreciated it must be viewed from close up, as the blending of the colors is very delicate. Turquoise possesses a beauty all its own, especially when it is mounted in silver.

Polishing Turquoise

Some amateur silversmiths are fortunate enough to live where cut and polished turquoise is available, and some can and do buy pieces of uncut or rough stone. Some have lapidary outfits to cut and polish the stones, and then there are those who are at a loss as to how they can cut and polish turquoise and other stones without buying new equipment. Cut and polished stones can be purchased from dealers. Anyone who would like to try cutting and polishing with little or no outlay of equipment, however, can do so by a simple method explained in the following paragraphs. All of the stones (turquoise) used in the neckerchief slides in Plate 24 were cut in this manner.

Most of the work can be done on a small hand grinder similar to the one in Figure 15. A power grinder as a rule runs too fast. Turning the hand grinder with one hand and manipulating the lap stick with the

FIG. 15. Rough grinding flat base on 4-in. carborundum wheel. Use side of wheel for final flat surface

other hand works very well, and it does not throw water all over the room. Those who have no grinding wheel may use a medium-rough abrasive cloth or paper, such as aluminum or carborundum, tacked to a board.

FIG. 16. Pieces of rough turquoise

Figure 16 shows rough turquoise. Select a piece, and grind off one side which will be the base or bottom. If carefully done, the stone can be ground dry, but a wet wheel prevents heating the stone so that it will not become too hot to hold. Heat also may discolor or crack the turquoise.

FIG. 17. Stone on lapstick. Rough grinding to desired shape

Wet the wheel, using a sponge or a squirt bottle like the one shown in Figure 15. Hold the rough stone against the wheel with your fingers, and grind off enough to make a good base. To do this, use the face of the wheel, and finish on the side to get it quite flat. Turn the grinder slowly and wet the wheel slightly every now and then. Too much water will cause splashing.

Now fasten the stone to a lap stick as shown in Plate 14, although this is not always necessary. Use wood dowel rod or wood skewers for lap or polishing sticks. Cement the stone to the lap stick with ordinary red sealing wax as shown at 1 and 2, Plate 14. Sealing wax and stick shellac melted together is somewhat stronger. The reason for applying the wax to the stone first is that this procedure will give better adhesion to the stone. The finished lap stick is shown at 6. Let the sealing wax cool before beginning to polish the stone.

With the rough stone on the stick, grind it down to the desired shape on the face of the wheel as shown in Figure 17. First grind away the high spots and gradually shape the stone. A coarse wheel cuts faster than a fine wheel but an ordinary small grindstone like those used on farms is ideal as they usually run in a trough of water.

Unless a definite shape of stone is desired, grind away only the rough part of the stone without wasting any of the good turquoise. The stone may be round, oval, square, oblong, or triangular, or any other pleasing shape. The idea is to get as much good stone out of the rough piece as possible with a minimum of waste.

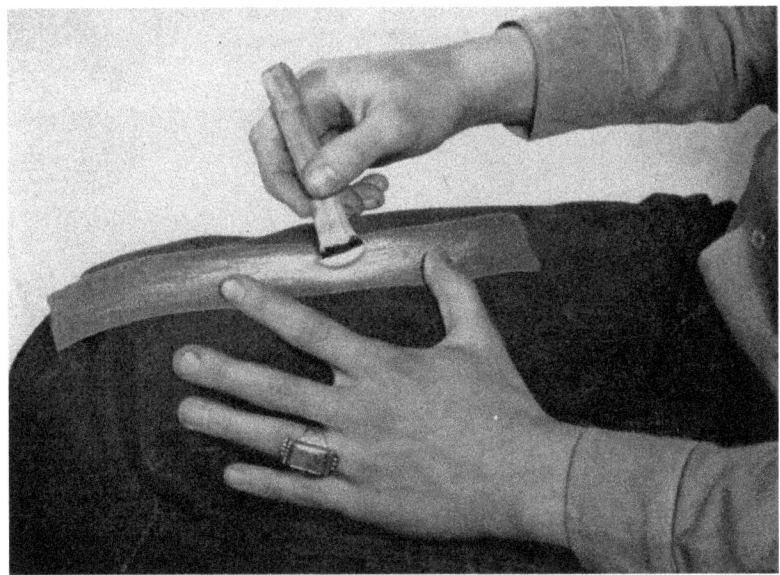

FIG. 18. Finishing grinding with 180-grit abrasive cloth held on knee

When the stone has been roughed out to where it has good lines, it is ready for the next step. This also may be done by more than one method. Either rub the stone on a sheet of 180-grit abrasive cloth placed on your knee, as shown in Figure 18, and work it back and forth, or use a *sandpaper stick* as shown in Figure 19. This stick is about 1½ in. wide and 10 to 12 in. long. Fasten a piece of sponge rubber to the stick and tack the abrasive cloth taut over that. Either way works out satisfactorily.

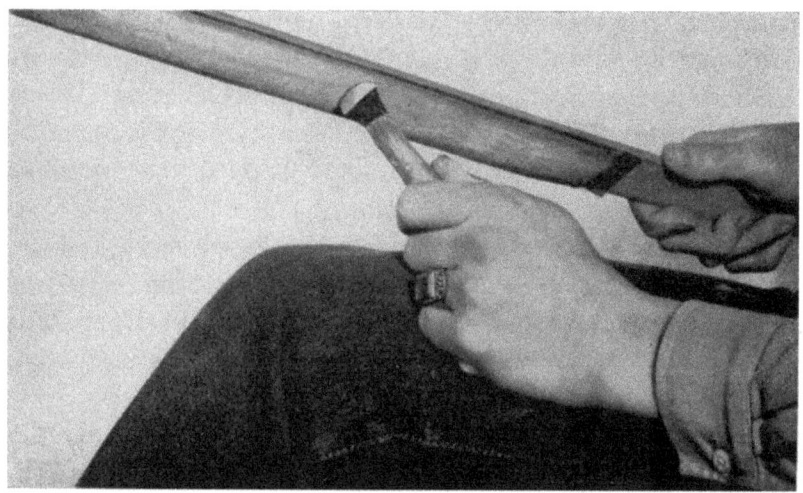

FIG. 19. Finish grinding with 180-grit abrasive cloth tacked onto stick over sponge rubber

Smooth the stone to a uniform surface. The abrasive cloth gradually wears down as it is being used, and it becomes quite smooth. The cutting action, therefore, becomes slower but finer.

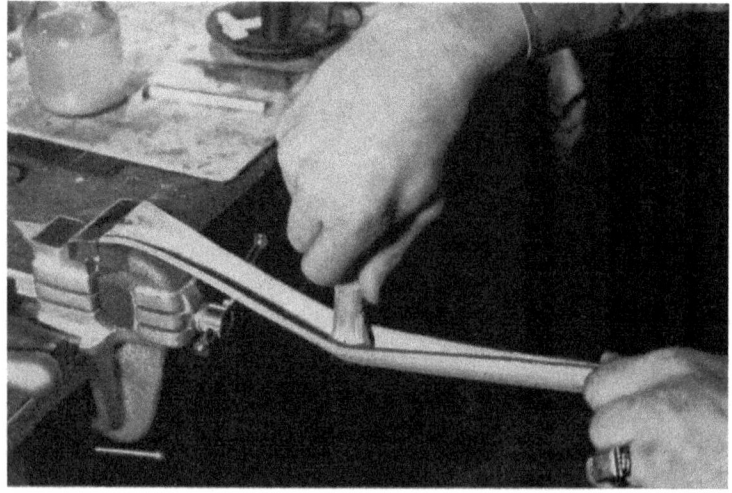

FIG. 20. Polishing with creamy paste of tin oxide on piece of heavy buckskin or other soft leather

The final step is the polishing. Either a heavy strip of canvas or a strip of heavy buckskin may be used. Figure 20 shows how the buckskin or polishing cloth is used. First, work paste of tin oxide into the buckskin. Tack one end to the edge of a table or clamp it in a vise and pinch the other end together. Rub the stone, which is still on the lap stick, vigorously back and forth in the trough thus formed. Keep turning while rubbing, and in a few minutes the stone will have a beautiful high polish.

Remove the stone from the stick by heating it as shown at the bottom of Plate 14, and twist it loose. Then, with a knife, cut away the wax left on the stone. Prying the stone loose with a knife may chip it, especially if the turquoise is of the soft variety. Malachite also can be handled in this manner as it has about the same degree of hardness as turquoise.

When grinding and polishing flat stones, do the fine grinding on 180-grit abrasive by tacking the abrasive on a flat hardwood board, *without having any rubber beneath it*. For the final polishing, also stretch and tack the polishing buckskin or canvas on a smooth hardwood board.

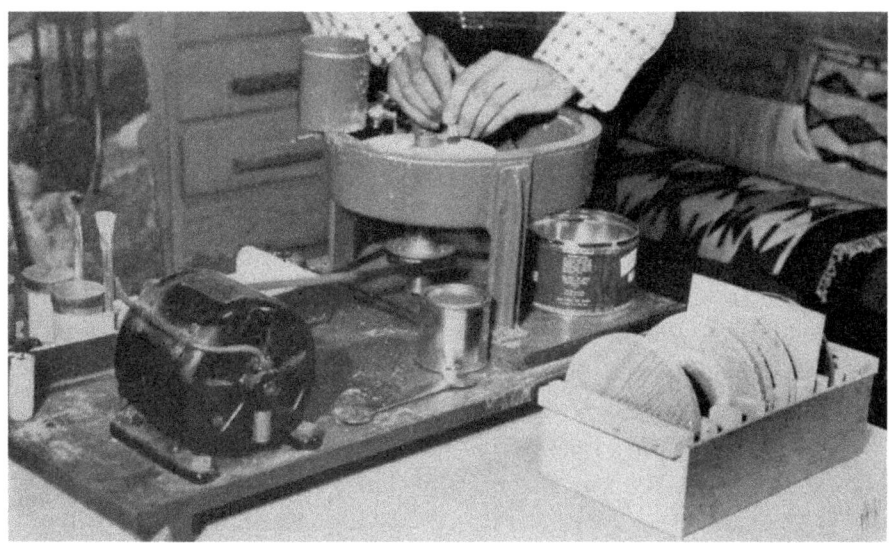

FIG. 21. Grinding on a small commercial lapidary wheel

Silver Bezels

BEFORE going into more intricate silversmithing, it may be well to discuss bezels because they play such an important part in the making of silver and turquoise jewelry. Bezels are made of 26 to 28-ga. sheet silver. Pure silver is best for this purpose because it is softer and does not melt so easily, but very few Indians use it. The regular sterling or coin silver, which is always on hand, is either hammered or rolled to the gauges mentioned. The thinner or 28-ga. is used for small bezels and the 26-ga. for the larger ones.

Regardless of the type or design of jewelry, if a stone is used a bezel is required, and its size is determined by the stone to be mounted. Plate 15 shows different kinds of bezels, and inasmuch as the general procedure in making a bezel is the same on most of them, the plain type in the upper left will be described. As stated before, the type and size of the stone determine the size of the bezel. Some stones, like the low cabochon, can be set high if so desired. This calls for a high bezel. A high cabochon can be set with a low bezel.

To begin, anneal the silver. If it is a long piece, coil it and place it on the soldering frame. Heat it to a cherry red and plunge it into cold water. This makes the silver soft and pliable. Straighten the silver and clean it with crocus cloth or fine pumice and water, or whiten it by immersing it in a hot pickle bath. Don't forget, however, to take off any iron wire that may be used in binding the silver before plunging the silver into the hot bath. Another method is to take off the iron wire, heat the bezel silver, and drop it into the cold pickle. The results are the same. Now twist one end of the silver around the stone to get the approximate size of the bezel, and cut off the surplus silver. Then form the bezel carefully to the shape of the stone, allowing just a little clearance, so that the stone will fit without being forced into the bezel. The ends of the bezel should butt together accurately to make a good solder joint. When a joint for a large bezel is being made ready for soldering, it sometimes is necessary to wire the bezel. However, experience will soon tell when and when not to use the binding wire.

There are two ways of soldering a joint. One method is to solder the joint first as a separate operation, and the other is to solder the joint and the bezel to the base in the same operation. To solder the joint first, proceed as when soldering a small ring, regardless of the size of the bezel. This is frequently done to insure a good fit. For most bezels up to ½ or ¾ in., it usually is advisable to solder the whole thing in one operation. A little experimenting should be done to see how each method works.

The bottom of the bezel must be a perfect fit on the base to which it is to be soldered. Uneven places can be taken down with a flat file. Place the solder snippets on the inside, about ¼ in. apart, and if the joint is to be soldered at the same time, lay a snippet against or over the joint on the inner side, as shown in the upper left-hand corner of Plate 15. The piece of solder for the joint should be at least as high as the bezel. Apply flux, and play the flame on the work, being careful not to heat the bezel more than the base or the solder will run *up* on the bezel. On the other hand, if the base is heated more than the bezel, the solder will run over it and not touch the bezel at all. When both are heated evenly, the solder will flow evenly around the base and along the joint. Remember to keep the parts clean.

Usually stones are mounted on level surfaces, but sometimes this is not practical. In that case, file the bottom of the bezel to fit the base or support. The top edge of the bezel always is level. When a stone is placed in such a bezel, first put a riser or support inside the bezel to give the stone a solid and level base all the way around. When mounting a low cabochon in a high bezel, also use this inner supporting ring. Sometimes, however, a piece of silver wire, bent to fit around the inside of the bezel, is enough to set the stone to the proper height. Very thin stones sometimes are cemented to a piece of phonograph record. In that case, file the record material to the shape and height desired. Be sure to set the stone

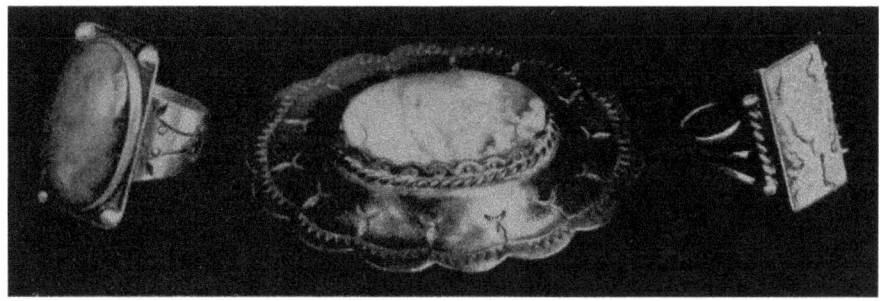

FIG. 22. Three kinds of bezels

Notice the high mounting on the brooch. A ring of wire was used for the riser, to set the stone higher

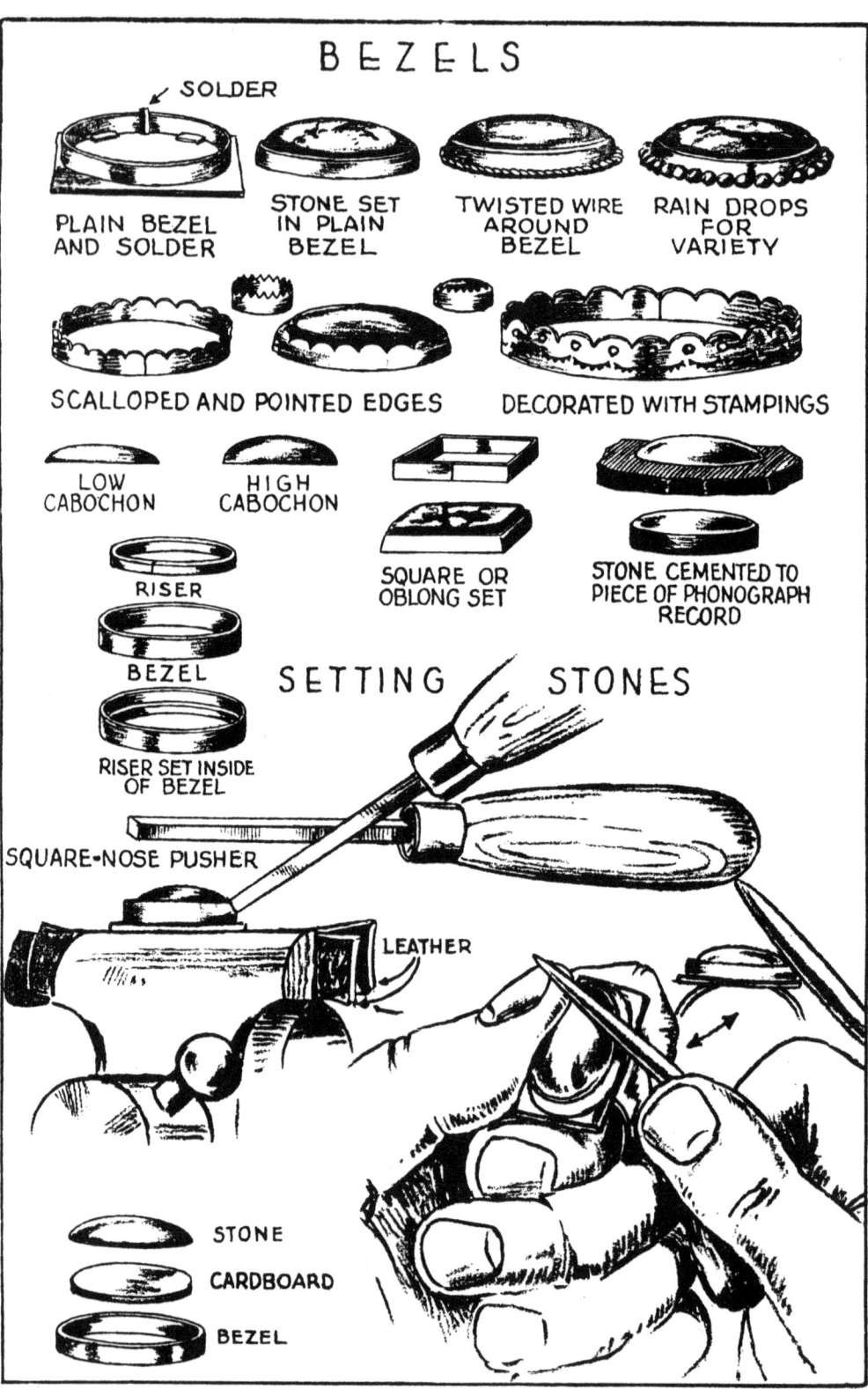

PLATE 15

so that none of the black record material can be seen, as shown in Plate 15. Set the stone into the bezel last, when everything else has been finished, since heat may ruin a stone and liver of sulphur may discolor it.

Another method of setting a stone is to cut a piece of blotting paper or cardboard to fit inside the bezel, as shown at the lower left in Plate 15. Set the stone over the cardboard into the bezel, and gently force the top of the bezel against the stone. This usually can be done with a smooth burnisher of hard steel or agate as shown at the lower right in Plate 15. Sometimes a pusher works better. In that case clamp the ring in a vise between two pieces of leather to prevent marring it, and push the edge of the bezel down evenly all around. It also may be necessary to use a small wooden mallet to force down the bezel. The upper edge should fit closely all around the stone. After using the pusher, even up the edge with a burnisher or smooth it with a small file. The cardboard is placed under the stone to take up any shock as it cushions the stone in the bezel.

For variety, filed edges on bezels are rather attractive. Filing usually is done before the bezel has been soldered and after the exact length of the metal has been ascertained. Before attempting the filing, straighten out the bezel and divide it evenly for scallops or points.

Rings Set With Turquoise

PLATE 16 shows 25 ring designs. Some of them were sketched from rings made by southwest Indians and the others were designed and made by the author. A few of them will bear a little explanation. In the ring in Number 1 the base of the bezel is curved to fit the finger better. That calls for an inner riser in the bezel to give the stone a flat surface on which to rest.

It is hard to show how ring Number 2 is constructed. The long, oblong base to which the bezels are soldered was laid on another larger piece of silver. This piece and the wire loops are of the 20 ga. B. & S. After soldering, the larger piece was filed or sawed away up to the wire loops.

The ring in Number 4 has no over-all base. The actual mount was constructed first. Then the twisted wires and the raindrops were laid together on a flat piece of charcoal or asbestos, and soldered. Any resulting unevenness was rectified by laying the soldered ring top on a level piece of metal and tapping it flat with a hammer over a piece of hardwood.

Numbers 7, 12, 13, and 19 show what can be done with odd-shaped stones.

Number 9 was made to fit a beautiful specimen of turquoise matrix which needed no other form of ornamentation. Number 10 shows a popular Navaho style of a man's ring. The band is made of three rings of round wire, similar to the band in Number 1.

Number 16 represents a Zuni sunset. The stone is half of a broken cabochon which required a little lapidary work. This is another example of what can be done with oddly shaped stones.

Number 18 is a sun symbol. The rays are pieces of silver wire rounded at the ends. To keep these wires from moving out of position during the soldering operation, lay them in a solution of gum tragacanth and water. This will not interfere with the flux, which is used in the regular way. Gum tragacanth can be bought at the prescription counter of almost any drugstore.

Number 19 is a green turquoise. Instead of the regular twisted wire, the

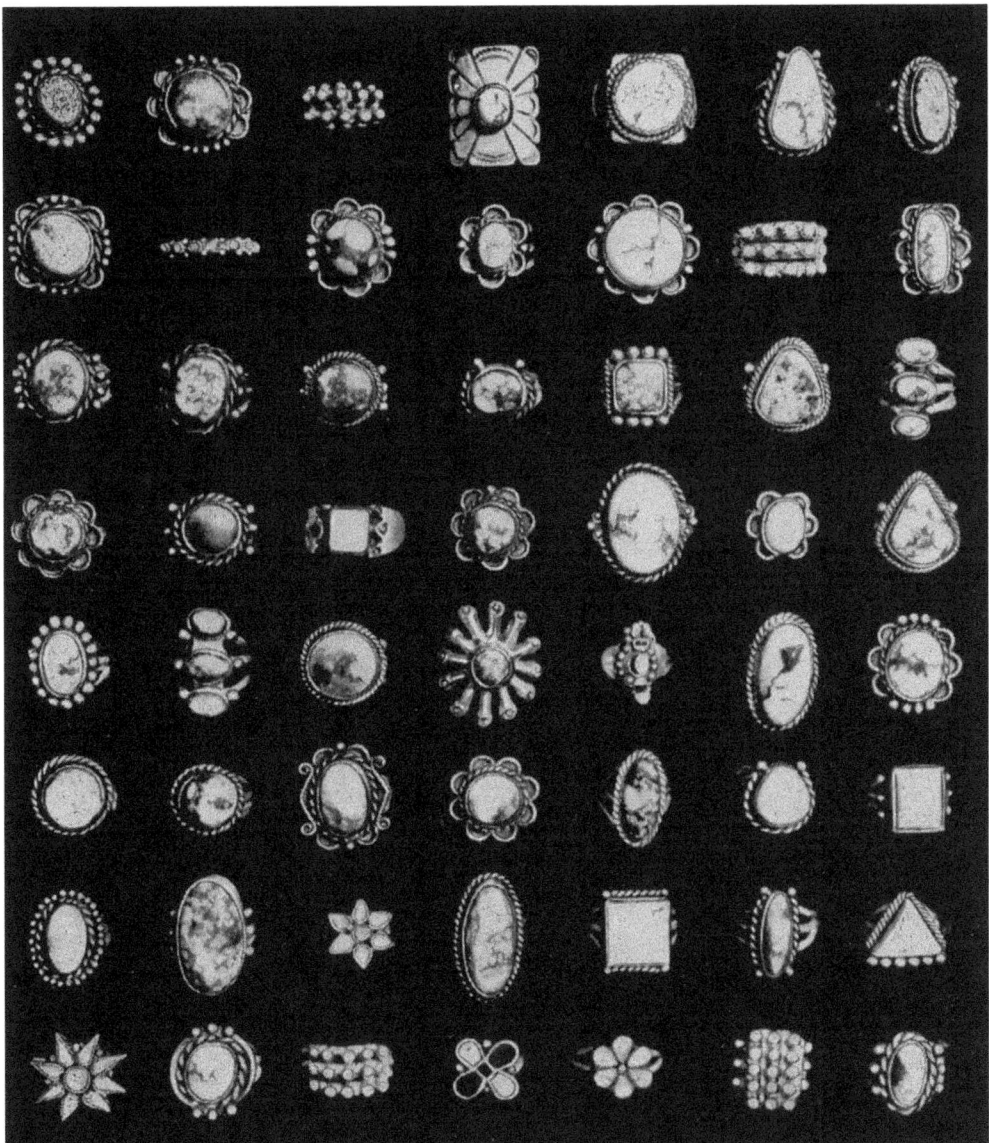

FIG. 23. Tray of Indian made rings photographed at the Turquoise Post, Santa Fe, N. Mex.

ornament was made of one strand of square wire, twisted rather tightly. The raindrops are very even in size and may have been bought ready made.

Number 22 shows a beautiful ring of two stones cut from the same shade of turquoise. An allover piece of silver was used for the base.

Number 25 is a ring set with petrified wood. The bezel, twisted wire, and raindrops were soldered to the base and the base was then sawed out and filed. This gives the whole top of the ring a more substantial support.

Turquoise matrix cracks easily when dropped or when hit by a hard object. A cracked stone usually is of no value unless it can be cut up and

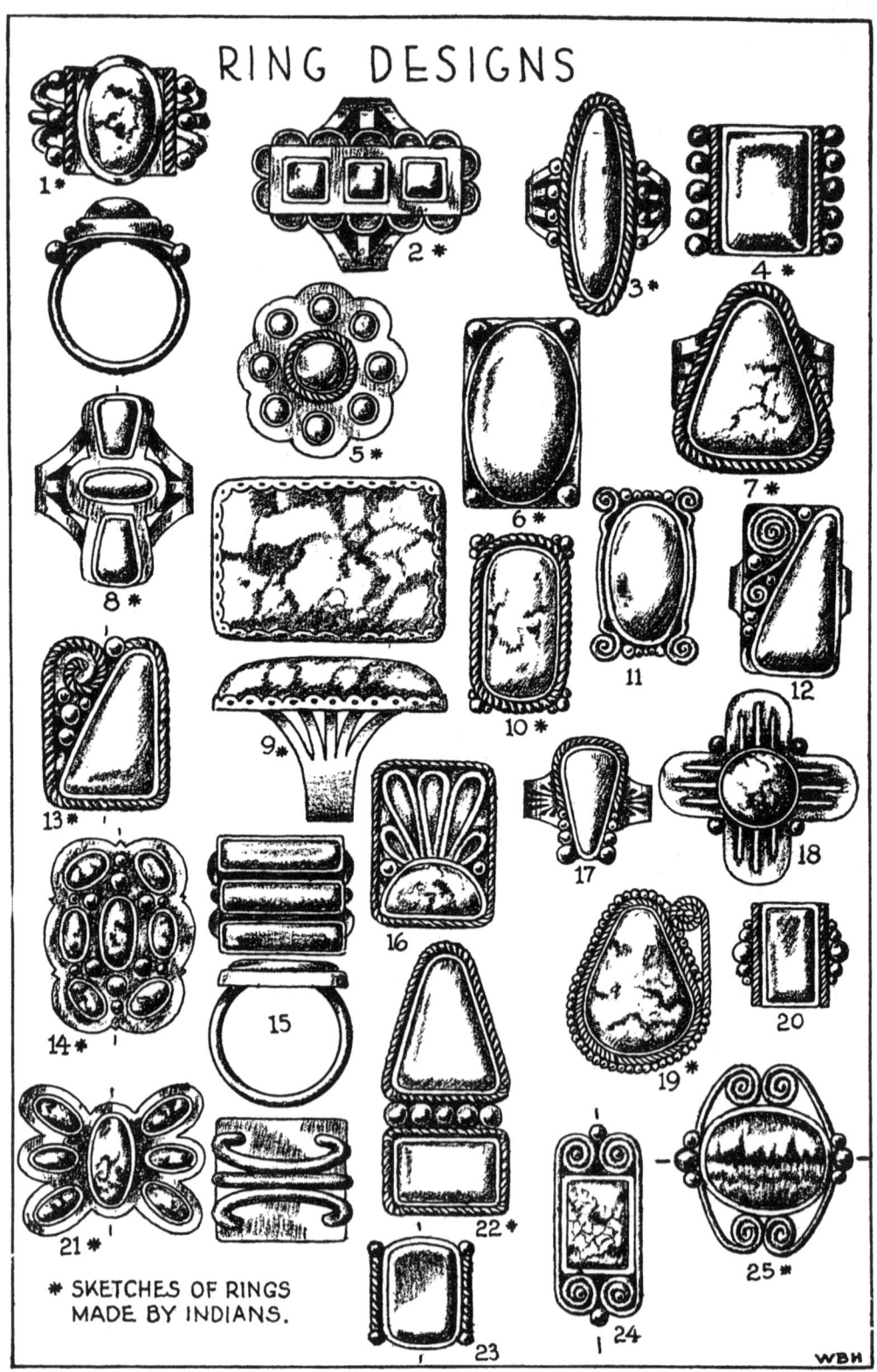

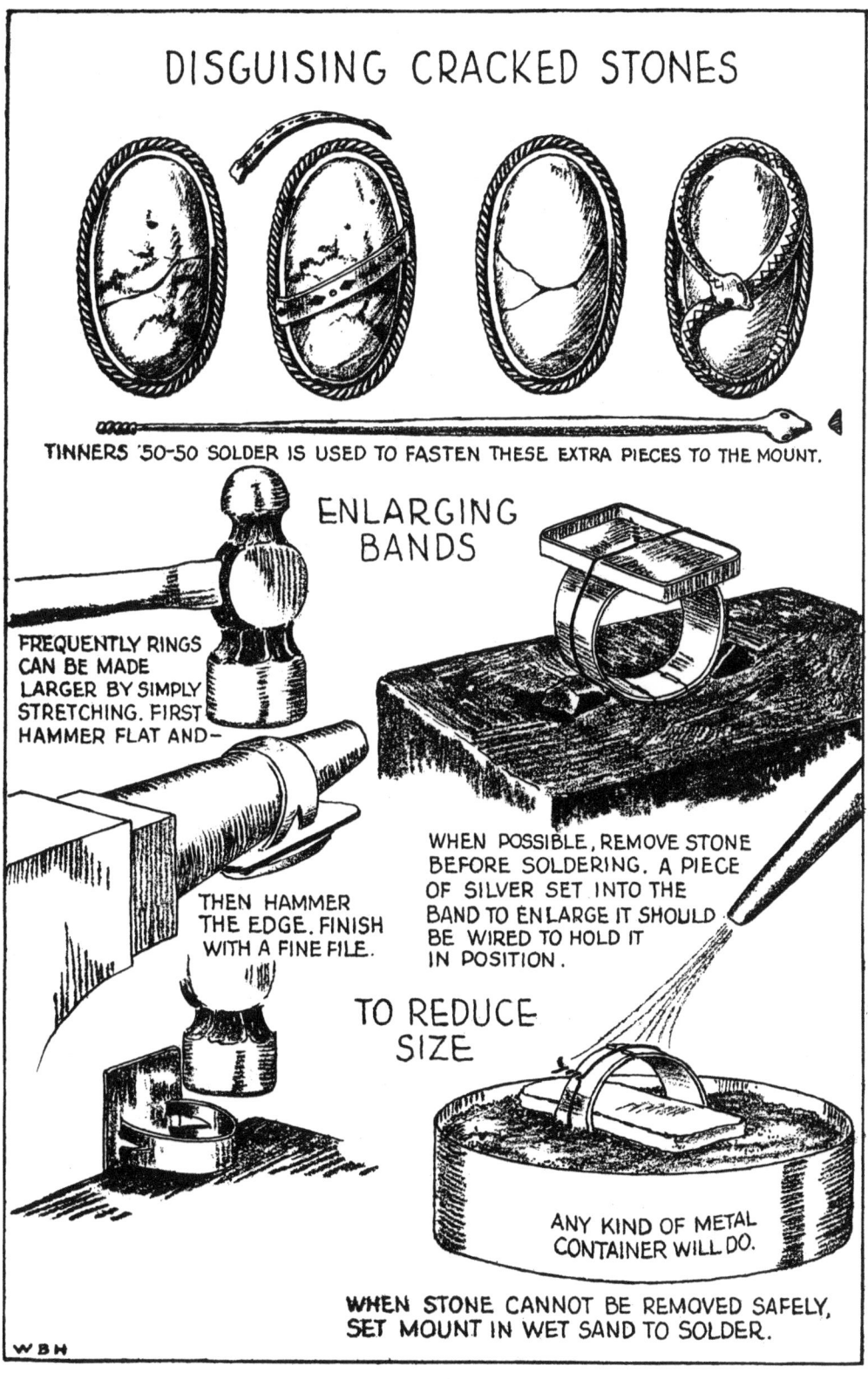

reground into smaller stones, or when the crack can be covered as shown in Plate 17. This sometimes adds to the attractiveness of the mount if done with a little thought and patience. A more or less straight fracture can be hidden by a straight bar wide enough to cover the crack. It should fit flush with the stone and the bezel. That can be done by carefully filing a groove for the bar. When properly fitted, the band is soldered to the bezel at each end with 50-50 tinner's solder and a small soldering copper. Do not use a flame as it will burn and discolor the turquoise, and do not use too much solder. Excess solder can be removed with a sharp knife, and since lead solder turns black in time it won't be noticeable.

In the second broken stone, a more elaborate covering must be used, and since rattlesnakes are quite common in the southwest, the snake would serve as an appropriate ornament. As shown below the rings, the snake first is hammered and filed to shape. The body is triangular in cross section and quite low. After shaping, stamp the crosshatching of diamond shapes along the back. Anneal the snake to be certain it will bend easily, and twist it to fit over the cracks and to lay perfectly flush with the setting. Then solder it with 50-50 tinner's solder where it touches the bezel or other silver.

A ring band can be enlarged by stretching the band on the horn of an anvil or some other round piece of metal as shown in Plate 17. Hammering spreads the metal in all directions. Hold the ring down tight to the horn. Then take it off the horn and hammer the edges to bring the width of the ring back to the proper size. Repeat if the ring has not stretched enough. File and polish for final finish.

When the difference is too great for stretching, saw the band through at the bottom, set in a piece of silver, and wire it in place as shown in Plate 17. After soldering, place the ring over an anvil horn or ring mandrel, and tap the joints carefully to even up any irregularities. Finish up by filing and polishing.

To remove a stone, run a sharp knife point around the inside of the bezel to spread it enough to take out the stone.

Sometimes it is not practical to remove old stones, and sometimes stones chip along the edges when running the knife point along them. In that case, *solder with 50-50 tinner's solder.* To play safe, pack the mounting in wet sand. *Remember that too much heat will crack or discolor turquoise.*

Left-hand row and top center: six bracelets; right-hand row, center: Hopi neckerchief slide. Rest of illustrations: brooches and pins.

Left: section of author's Navaho-made concha belt; top right: keto; right: three belt buckles described in text.

Men's Rings

THE two rings shown in Plate 18 resemble the heavy cast rings made by the Indians, but they are much lighter in weight. This is an advantage, because cast rings, especially large ones, if they do not fit snugly, roll or slide over to one side of the finger.

The ring with the turquoise setting in Plate 18 and Figures 24 and 25 was made in one afternoon and the other ring was made in an evening. This included the cutting and polishing of the stone.

To make the ring in 1, Plate 18, proceed as follows. First, make the ring band shown in 2, Plate 18. The pattern is slightly larger at the top to allow for good soldering, and the surplus silver is filed off later. Make the ring band the correct size and solder it, provided no stamping is done. Then cut the bezel, 3, Plate 18, to see how closely it fits over the band. Do not solder it. When a fairly good fit has been obtained, flatten the bezel again and stamp it as shown in 3, Plate 18. Next, bend it to shape again over a mandrel, and solder the ends as shown in 4. Then comes the final fitting. File it as shown in 10, Plate 18, until it fits perfectly flat on the top of the band. The tapered sides of the bezel can be seen in Figures 24 and 25. When the bezel has been fitted closely, wire and

FIG. 24. The oval ring with turquoise setting and the other before setting the malachite. The padding of phonograph record material is not shown. FIG. 25. The finished rings

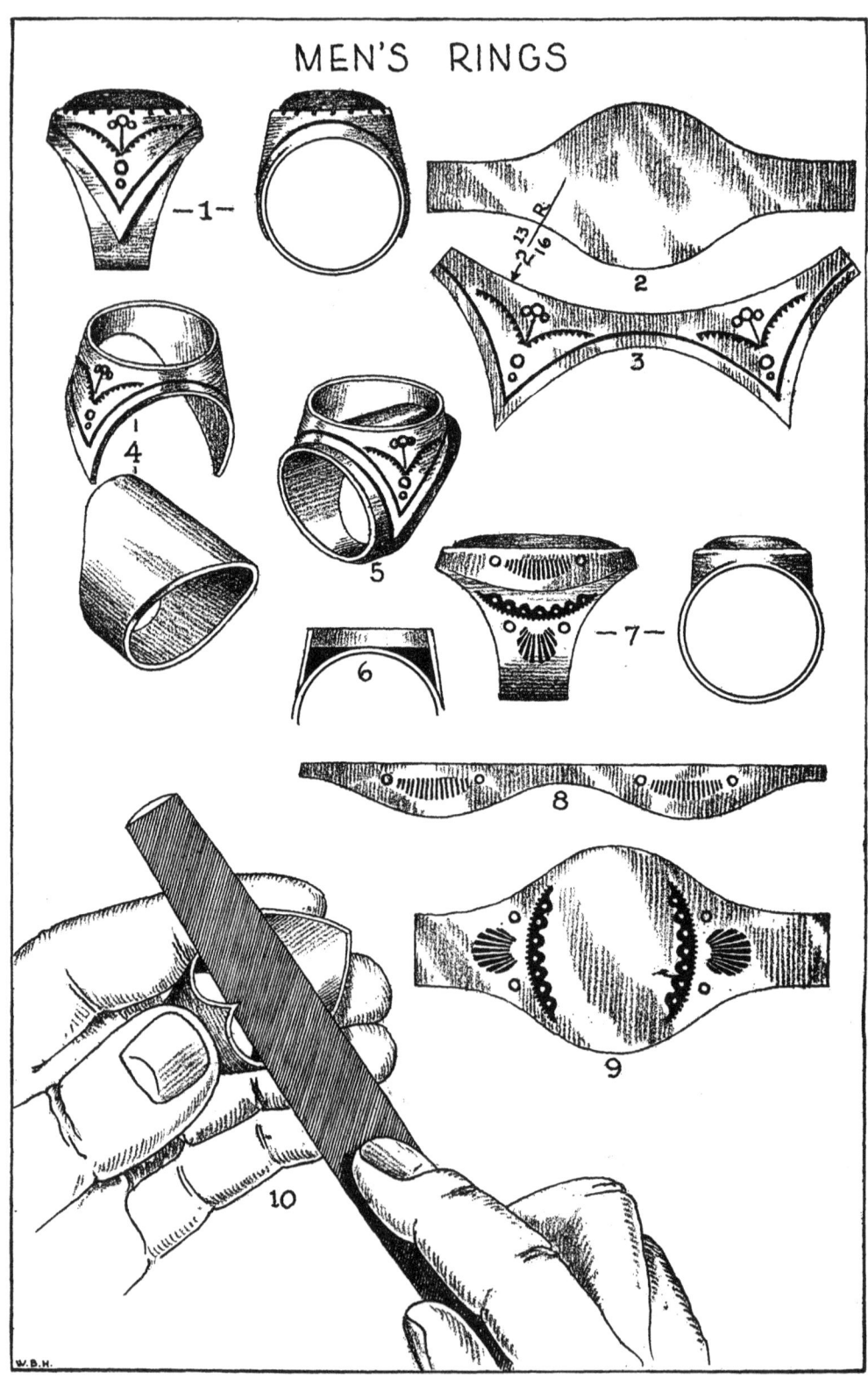

PLATE 18

solder it, placing the solder snippets inside of the bezel. After soldering, file away the surplus.

There are two ways of forming a base for the stone. For the ring with the oval turquoise, solder a flat plate inside the bezel for the stone to rest on. To form the bed for the stone in the other ring, clamp the ring in a vise, and place pieces of a broken phonograph record into the bezel. Then carefully heat the ring until the phonograph-record material becomes soft, and press it down to form a flat base for the stone. Number 6, Plate 18, shows the phonograph base.

The bezel in the ring in 7, Plate 18, has straight sides. The same procedure is followed in making this ring as the one just described. Make the band first, and bend it over a mandrel as though ready for soldering. Cut out the bezel, bend it to fit the stone, and file it to fit the band. Hold it in place on the band, and mark where it fits. These marks will indicate where the ring is to be stamped. Straighten out the band and stamp it. Next, solder the band and then the bezel. After soldering the bezel, bend it carefully to fit the stone. File the bezel to fit, and wire and solder it to the band. Next, if so desired, solder a flat piece of silver or thin copper for the base of the stone or make a bed of phonograph-record material as previously described. File off the surplus silver, and polish and set the stone.

In making the ring in 1, Plate 18, the stone was cut to fit the setting. The notches in the bezel are filed as shown in Figure 11. Eighteen-gauge silver is used for the bands and 20-ga. for the bezels. To make the setting of the stones easier, file down the edges of the bezel.

PLATE 19

Channel Work

CHANNEL work in Indian silversmithing made its first appearance about 1928. There was not much demand for this type of jewelry, however, until about 1946 when good turquoise had become scarce.

For channel work the Indian uses chips and small flat fragments of turquoise which are easily ground to shape. Plate 15 shows how a thin polished piece of turquoise can be cemented to a piece of phonograph record to give it more height. In channel work this can be readily done and consequently even the thinnest fragments of turquoise can be utilized. A great deal of simulated turquoise is being used. It has a beautiful deep color, and although it is an imitation, the price is the same as the genuine. This imitation turquoise usually can be detected by its coloring which is too even and too perfect. Simulated turquoise sometimes dissolves in lacquer thinner or banana oil. The slight variations in the color of real turquoise and the slight unevenness of the silverwork are what make Indian jewelry so attractive.

Plate 19 shows a flat ring at the upper left-hand corner. It also shows how the setting is soldered. To make a ring like this, first shape the outer rim with sharp corners, then fit the two long dividers, and finally the six short dividers. It takes quite a bit of filing and fitting. Then solder the box, or housing, and finally solder the band to it. Cut the stone with a sandpaper stick or on a carborundum wheel. Use a lap stick to hold the stone, because that is much safer than trying to hold it with the fingers. Get skewer sticks from the butcher to make small lap sticks, and whittle out the larger ones. Flatten the good side of the stone first and fasten that side to the stick with sealing wax. Now comes the more difficult step, that of grinding it to shape on a carborundum or silicon wheel. Fit the stone as shown in the sketch below the lap stick. If the turquoise is thick enough for the housing it will look like A in Plate 19. If it is a thin piece, press it into a heat softened piece of phonograph record, as shown at B, and let it cool. Then cement the two together; while that is drying, proceed with the next piece. After the cement has dried, file the stone to shape, trying it frequently for size. Try to get a snug fit, and the top or face of the stone should be *above* rather than below the housing. A small piece of beeswax may be used to hold small stones for fitting. When the proper fit has been obtained, put cement on the stone, push it down in place, and let it dry. When *all* the pieces have set, grind off the entire face carefully, down to the channels, taking off a little of the silver. Do the finish grinding with a piece of medium-grit carborundum cloth tacked to a piece of wood. Sometimes the grinding pulls the silver over the stone enough to hold it securely, but sometimes a burnisher must be used to slightly flatten or spread the edge of the housing. The housing, which is in reality the bezel, is not crimped over the stone as in other settings.

In the shaped ring, another method is followed. The two end pieces marked X are filed where they fit onto the band. The shaping and fitting of the stones also is a little more difficult.

The lower earring is made of five round housings and four flattened raindrops set between the outer housings. Much solder is used, and after all has been ground down there is no evidence of the rings holding the stones except where shown on the outside.

The bracelets are all soldered together flat, and then slowly shaped before the stones are set. Note that the ends are flat beyond the housings except for the lower bracelet which has a half-round rope wire soldered along the edges.

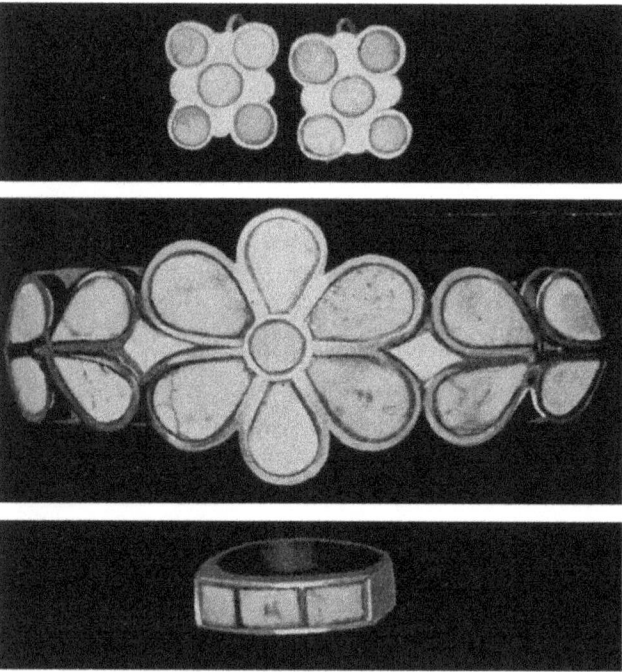

FIG. 26. Earrings, bracelet, and ring made with channel work

Ear Ornaments

THE ear ornaments in Plate 20, made of scrap metal, are fine one-evening jobs and excellent practice in soldering. If anything goes wrong, this scrap metal can be melted and used again.

By soldering these small parts, a beginner will acquire the feel for proper heating when he is ready to solder larger pieces, or when he has to join small pieces to those of larger size.

Four new stamps are shown in this plate. These will be found useful in making the ear ornaments.

Plate 3 shows how stamps are made. The two stamps shown in the lower right hand in Plate 20 are rather interesting. At Q is shown the punch used to make the little round holes. The point of the punch should be reground to a somewhat sharper angle than that used on a center punch.

These stamps are made of drill rod, shaped roughly, and punched with the reground punch. Locate the place for each hole with a light punch mark, and hammer a little harder until the holes are as they should be. The punch will push up the metal around the holes. File these elevations carefully until an even surface again has been obtained. Hammer a little more and file until the surface is smooth again. Make stamp R by drilling out the center, and then filing the radial cuts. A and B show different stampings on the same shaped background.

FIG. 27. Stamp the design before cutting out the blank

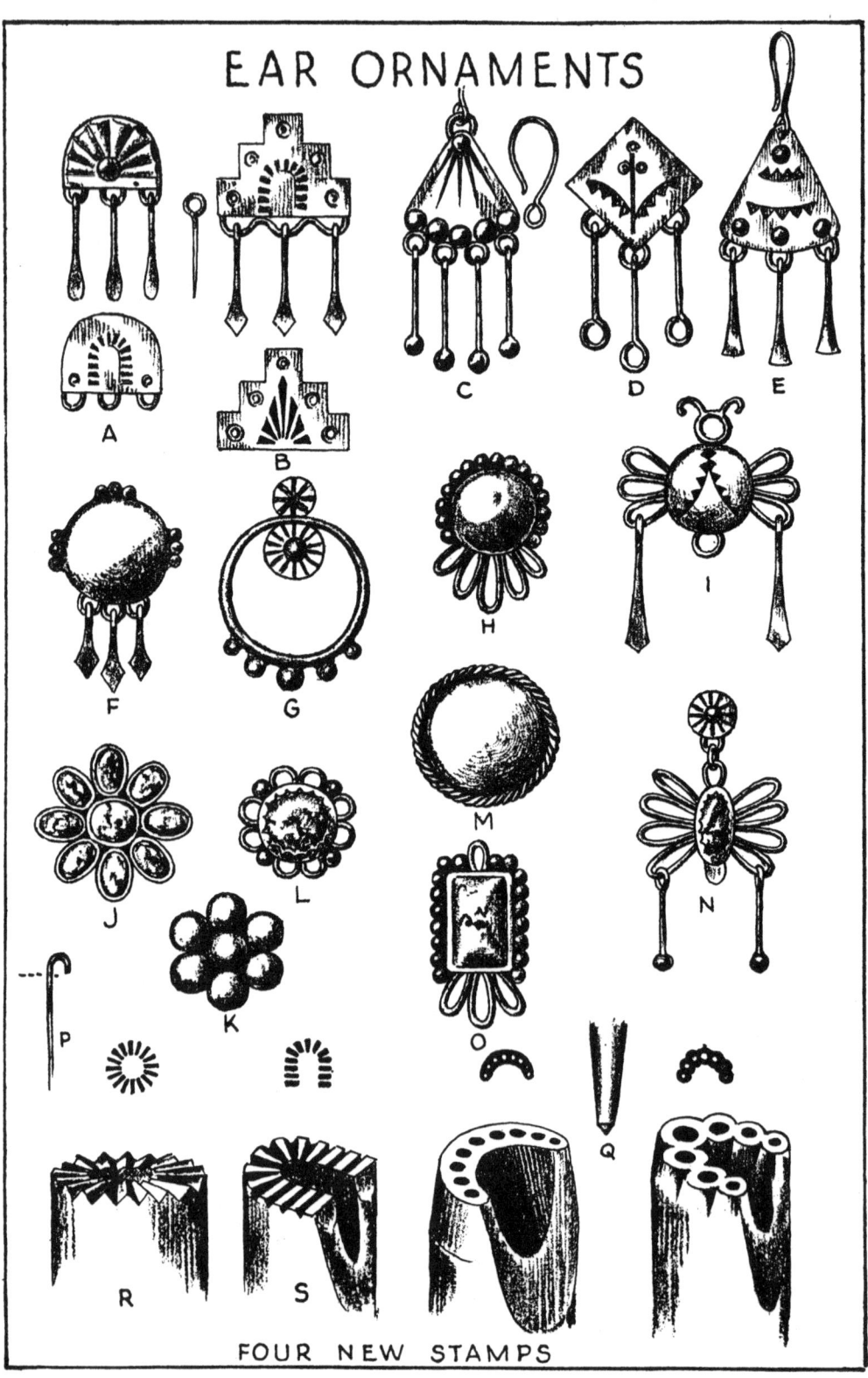

PLATE 20

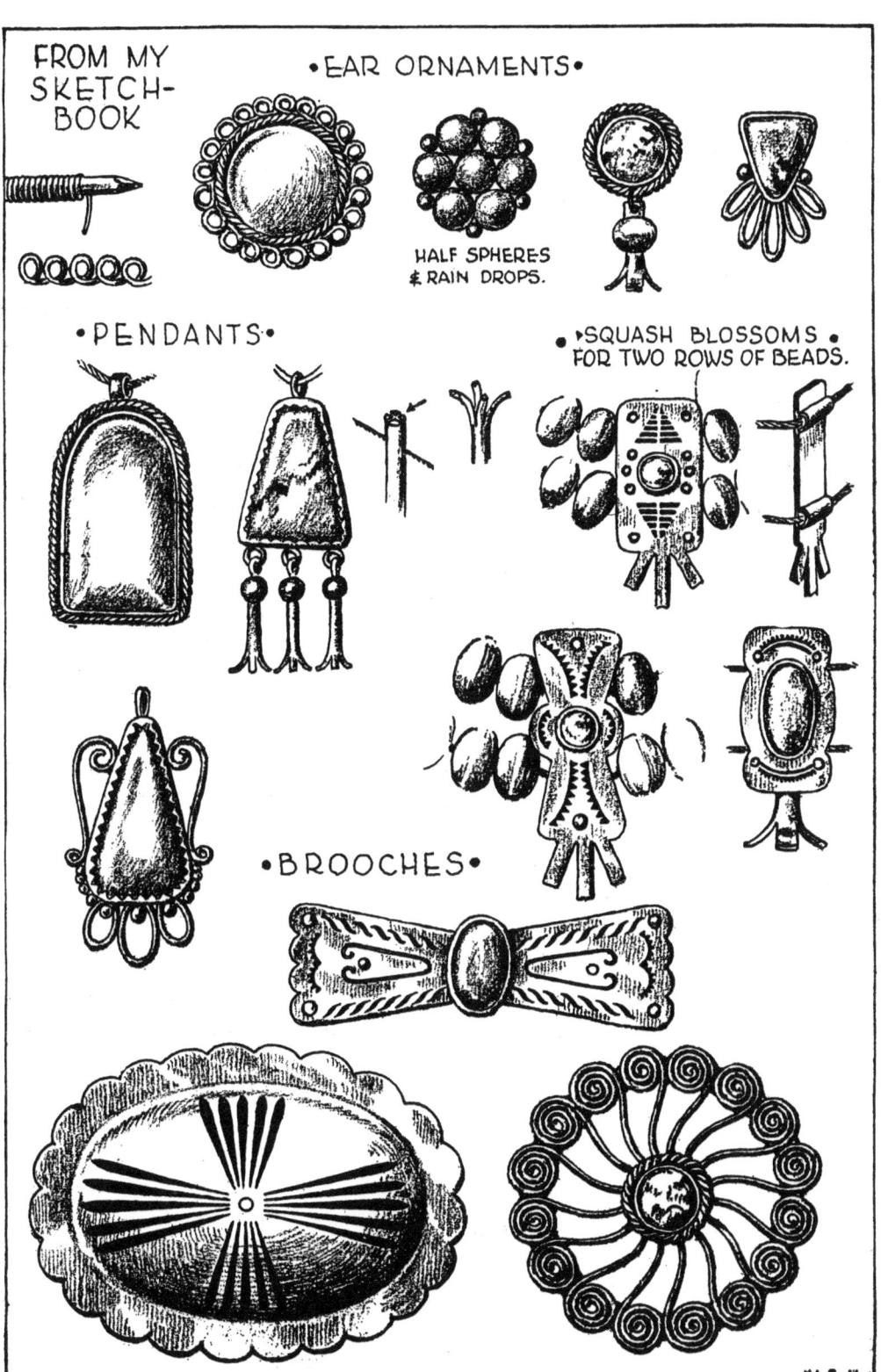

PLATE 21

All of the ear ornaments, A, B, C, D, and E, are made according to the same general plan; that is, a flat piece of 20-ga. silver with wire spangles. Mark the shape on the scrap piece of silver with a pencil and stamp the design on it before cutting out, as shown in Figure 27. On small pieces, stamping is done before cutting because small pieces of silver have a tendency to spread. Cut the pieces to the outline, almost to the inner corners with a small tin snips and then break off the pieces. A few strokes of a file will dress up the blank. Turn it face down, on a smooth anvil or block of wood, and hammer it level. Twenty-gauge wire is used. First, bend the wire loops as shown at P, Plate 20, and then cut them off. File all loops to fit snugly against the main piece. The upper ornament at B, Plate 20, shows another way of making the loops. Some of the ornaments have *raindrops*. When making these raindrops, even if exactly the same amount of silver is used, there will be some variation in size. To make the raindrops uniform, place them in one of the small depressions in the dapping die, with the flat side up, as shown at A, Plate 5. Then tap them down into the depression, and run a file over the flattened part. As a result, they will also set firmly on whatever they are to be soldered.

When soldering a number of articles at the same time and not all are satisfactory, put a drop of flux on the metal without cooling it. Then put another little snippet of solder over the joint, heat those parts again, and they will be soldered perfectly.

The ornament at G, Plate 20, has nine places to be soldered. Two of these ornaments may be soldered at one time, by having them on a charcoal block, side by side. As soon as one is soldered, move the flame over and solder the second one. Stamp the disk on the inside of the wire ring in ornament G with stamp R, and solder a raindrop to the center of it. Set the raindrops at the bottom up against the ring with a small snippet of solder where they touch the ring.

Make the wire spangles last. Flatten and shape the ends of the wire, and cut off a ⅞-in. length from the long piece. Bend the eye, open it again, put it in place, and then close it.

The spherical parts in ornaments F, H, I, K, and M, Plate 20, are hammered out on a dapping die. See B, C, D, and E, Plate 5. All have backs soldered to them after they have been shaped and filed. B, Plate 5, shows how to file the edges of these little half spheres by setting them in a dapping block depression. The shallow parts of spheres can be made by using a larger depression as shown at C, Plate 5. When using the dapping block, do not file the block.

J, Plate 20, shows a Zuni design with eight turquoise stones. Solder the bezels onto a flat piece of silver, cut the surplus metal away with a jeweler's saw, and then file. Follow the same procedure with K.

When making the *bug* ear ornament shown at I, Plate 20, stamp the body before shaping it in the dapping die. Then solder a back to the domed piece, and follow with the wings, head, feelers, and tail. Ornaments L, N, and O, Plate 20, have turquoise centers. The ear ornaments in Figure 28 were photographed before the clasps were soldered on, to make photographing a little more simple. Both silver and white metal clasps can be purchased from handcraft shops and in some department-store notion departments. The pair shown are of white metal and can be fastened to the body of the ornament with soft solder. Use 50-50 tinner's solder and the same flux and one or two small snippets of solder. Using soft solder eliminates the danger of the solder in the earring melting, as the melting point of the silver solder is much higher. Indians usually have their ears pierced and then use the simple hooks shown on the ornament at E, Plate 20.

Beginners should be very careful when soldering hollow domes to flat bases. Small domes can be easily soldered, but occasionally, when soldering domes over ⅜ in. in diameter, the heat expands the air inside and prevents the solder from making a perfect joint along the edge. Then, when the soldered piece is placed in the pickle, the acid is drawn into the hollow center and is difficult to remove. Be sure to have a perfect solder joint *all* around the domed pieces.

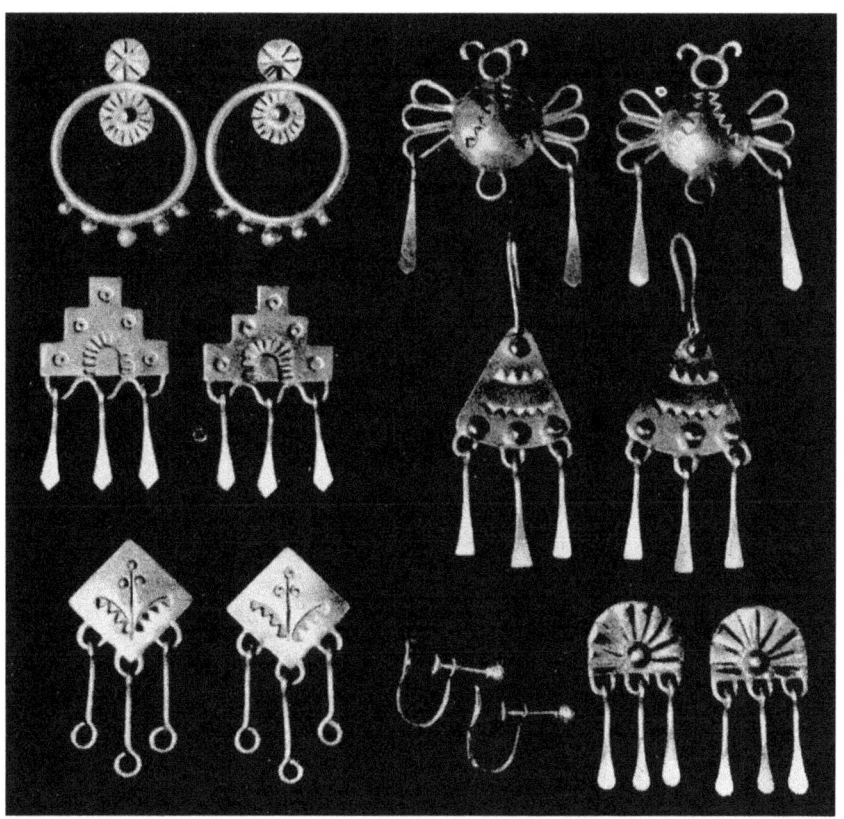

FIG. 28. Finished ear ornaments

PLATE 22

Brooches

INDIANS, as a rule, do not wear brooches, and consequently these pieces of ornamentation are rather scarce, since they are mostly made on order. The brooches in Plate 22 are sketches of brooches seen in the southwest as well as the author's own design.

Number 1, Plate 22, is simply a flat base with settings and stampings. In 2, the inner oblong is bumped up, enclosed by a border of twisted wire, and an oblong stone is mounted in the center. This brooch will be just as attractive without the stone if the bumping up is neatly done and the entire brooch is polished. Brooch 3 has a scalloped bezel and wire ornamentation. The brooches in 4 and 5 were made by the author. The one in 5 was bumped up, and is very beautiful even though it has no stone. The brooch in 6 is bumped up. When bumping or doming, all irregularities must be taken out with a fine file and the domed piece given a high degree of polish before it is soldered to the base. After the twisted wire has been soldered around these domes, the amount of polishing required usually cuts away a lot of the wire, and even then it is impossible to polish the edges properly.

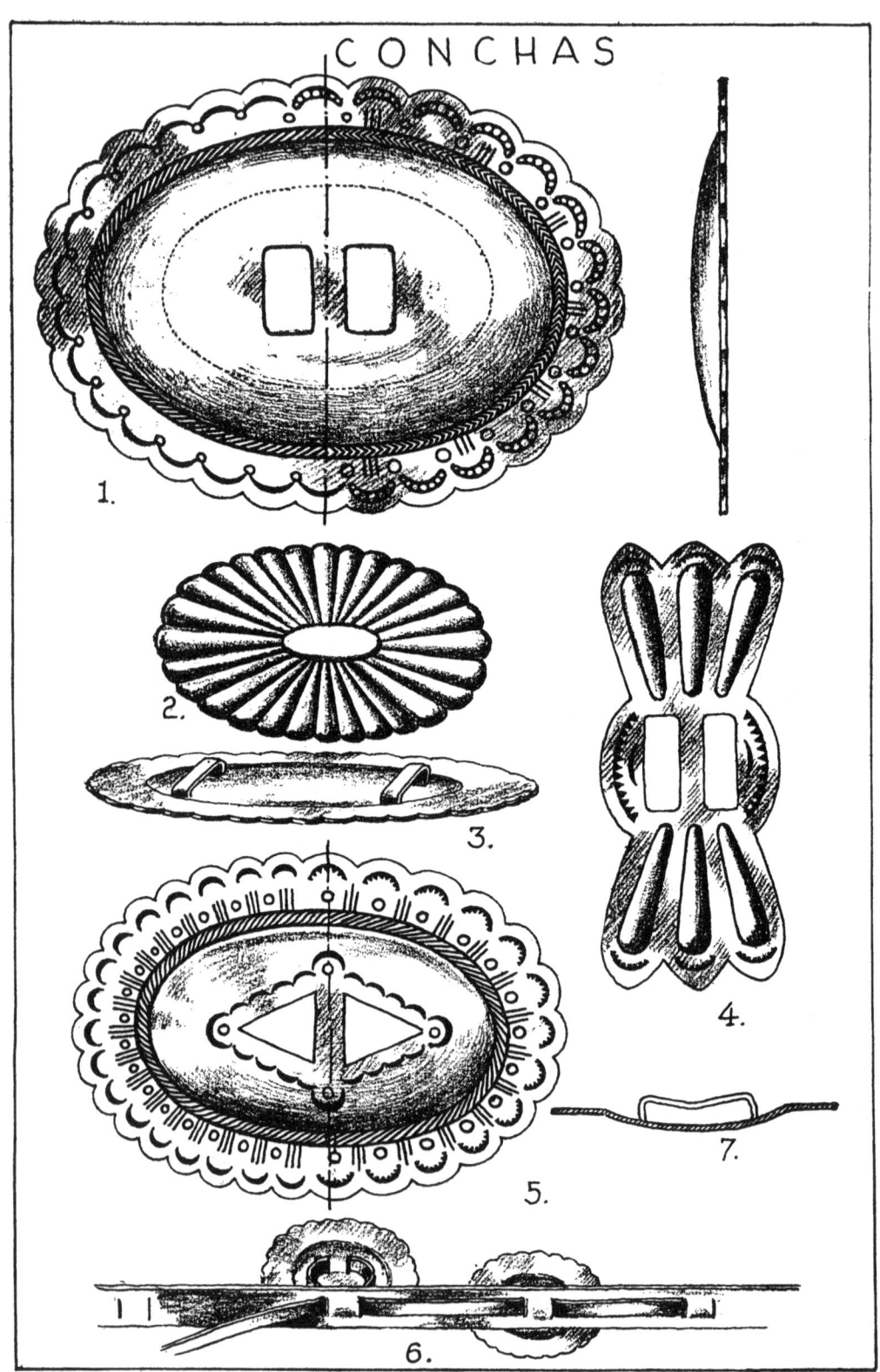

PLATE 23

Concha Belts

SILVER concha belts are the most expensive pieces of jewelry made by the Navaho Indians, and worn only by those who can afford to buy or make them. Before Indians learned to do silver soldering and set turquoise, conchas were made similar to the ones shown in 1 and 5, Plate 23, rather plain and of heavy silver. They are simple in form and easily made. In this type of concha belt, the strap is drawn through the opening and sometimes is laced to a wider and heavier strap, as shown in Number 6. Figures 29 and 30 show that some of the belts have wide straps and some have a single narrow strap. Butterflies, as shown in 4, Plate 23, often are placed between the conchas.

After the Indians learned how to solder, the appearance of the conchas changed, as shown in Figures 29 and 30. The majority of these conchas have a fluted sunburst in the central raised part and some are set with turquoise. These conchas usually are made with a punch and die. The punch is filed to shape first, and hardened. Then another piece of iron is heated to a white heat and the punch is hammered into it. This requires many repeated heatings and stampings until the entire face of the punch has been sunk into the die. The Indian does not take into consideration the amount of clearance to allow for the metal being stamped, and consequently, some conchas have holes torn into the flutings, caused by the lack of clearance.

When complete dies are not available, the sunburst is fluted by hammering up each section separately. Such conchas are readily noticed by the smaller or greater number of irregularities. Some belts have sunbursts which vary from 24 to 27 separate flutes. The large, beautiful concha belt in Figure 29 was originally made of old-type conchas, and the sunburst was added later. This fluted sunburst is not bumped up, but is comparatively easy to make, as described in previous chapters. Sunbursts with wide fluting can be bumped out on the concha, but those on the center belt in Figure 29 were made similar to the one in 1, Plate 23. These sunbursts were made by hammering down the radial lines in rather heavy silver and

FIG. 29. Examples of concha belts

FIG. 30. Examples of buckles used on concha belts

Rings, buttons, watch band, necklaces, earrings, and turtle pins. Most of these articles are described in this book.

Part of Stan. Hildebrand's collection of choice turquoise and crysocola.

filing the flutings. The ends then were rounded and scalloped with a file and the bottom filed smooth. The top view of such sunburst is shown at 2, Plate 23. It is hammered or bumped up in the same wooden form used to bump up the concha and then is soldered in place.

Most of the concha belts are made along similar lines. The buckles, however, are of all styles and shapes, and in some cases do not match the conchas used on the belt.

After the sunburst has been bumped up, the rest of the concha is not difficult to make. First, cut out the oval and file the edges. Next, with dividers or by finger gauging, lay out the line to mark the edge of the bumped-up section and a second line outside of it to mark the width of the rope design, that is, if a rope border design is used. Stamp the rope design. Decide on the design for the border. Divide the oval in quarters with a pencil, lay out the spacing for the border stamping, and stamp the design. Next, file the scallops to conform with the half-moon stampings.

If the concha to be made is of the old style, shown in 1 and 5, Plate 23, cut two openings for the belt, with a small sharp chisel or with a jeweler's saw. Finish the openings with a file. Bump up the center on a block of wood hollowed out to the desired depth, raising the center about ¼ in. After bumping up, turn the concha face up and tap down the rim with a piece of wood and a hammer, or by going around the inner line of the rope design with a lining tool. File any irregularities in the domed part.

The sunburst design in Figure 30 has no openings for the strap, but must be shaped, stamped, filed, and bumped up as previously described, after which it is soldered in place on the concha.

To make the butterfly in 4, Plate 23, outline the flutes with a lining tool, bump them up from the bottom, turn them face up, and tap along the outlines again to flatten the rim. Repeat until the fluted parts are high enough.

The old-style conchas do not require loops for the belt strap, but the new styles do. The loops are made of copper about ¼ in. wide. Two loops are required for the concha in 3, Plate 23, and one for the butterfly. These loops should be a little narrower than the belt strap so they will not slip. Solder the loops in place, and if they show a tendency to slip on the belt strap, press the center down as shown in 7, Plate 23.

The conchas are either strung on a narrow strap or as shown in 6, Plate 23. The wide belt often is as wide as the conchas, as shown in some of the belts in Figure 30.

The making of buckles is shown in Plates 34, 35, and 36. A number of ideas for buckles also may be obtained from Figures 29 and 30.

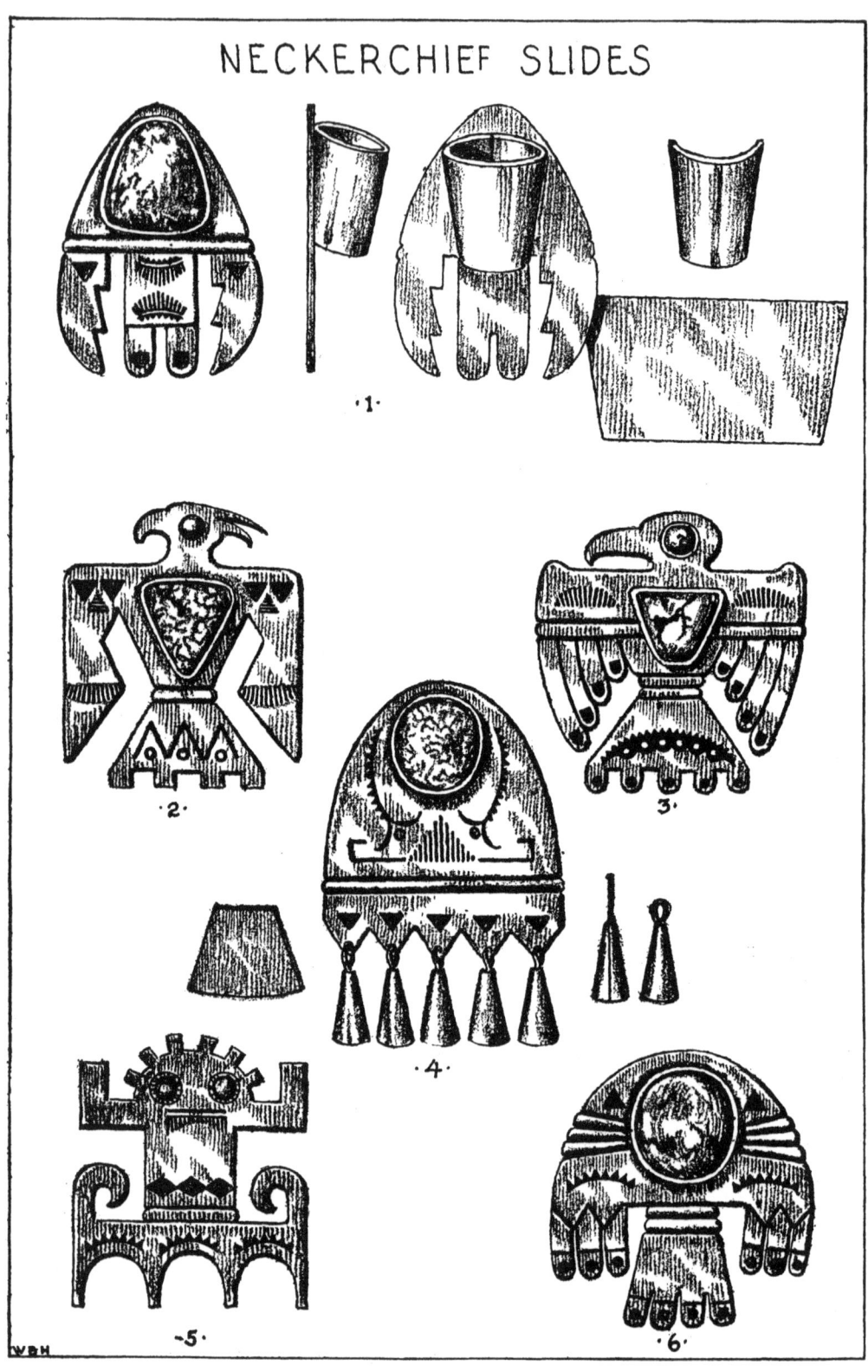

PLATE 24

Neckerchief Slides

NECKERCHIEF slides are quite modern in Indian silversmithing. They are not often seen in shop showcases, but when worn they never fail to attract attention. In scouting, neckerchief slides are standard equipment and are made out of almost anything to which a loop can be fastened. The slides in Plate 24 have small loops and are used on the small, triangular silk neckerchiefs and on regular neckties. They can, however, be made with larger loops, ¾ in., to be worn with large neckerchiefs.

To make a slide, anneal a piece of silver and dip it in pickle to whiten it. Then draw or trace the design onto the silver and do the stamping first, after which saw out the design with a jeweler's saw. In this way the lines in the design remain even. If the design were stamped after the piece was sawed out, the lines might spread.

In 1, Plate 24, is shown the construction of an Indian-made slide set with turquoise. It has a full round loop, but a half loop as shown at the right is better. Loops may be of copper. Eighteen- or twenty-gauge silver

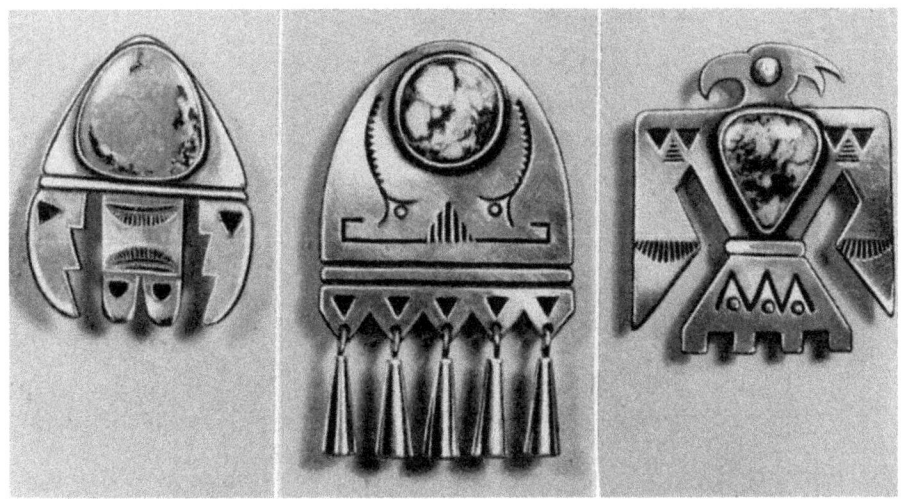

FIG. 31. Finished neckerchief slides

can be used for the front and twenty-four gauge for the loop. In 2, Plate 24, a raindrop is used for the eye, while 3 has a small turquoise.

An attractive slide requiring a little more work is shown in 4, Plate 24. Cut out and shape the cone pendants around a nail set with pliers and a hammer. Insert the wire, and solder the seam and wire on a charcoal block. Then bend the wire in the shape of an eye, hook it in place on the slide, and close the eyes.

Number 5 shows a slide without turquoise.

In 4 and 6, Plate 24, a half dome of sheet metal may be soldered on instead of a turquoise, and a twisted wire may be soldered around the edge of the dome, as shown in Figure 32. Use a full-round loop on slide 4 as the slide should hang a little forward to give the pendants a chance to hang free.

The loops may be made of copper if desired, especially when making several slides, because it is cheaper and thus is quite a saving.

When no turquoise is available, copper may be used for the bumped-up dome. In that case, do not use the twisted wire as the solder may run up onto the dome. To prevent the solder from running, file the bottom of the dome so it lies flat. File off the burr, but be careful not to file up on the dome. Flux the flat, and lay the dome down on the wet flux. Then place small snippets of solder around the edge, and apply the heat. When the melting temperature has been reached, the solder will flow in place without spreading onto the dome.

FIG. 32. Made with bumped up half sphere and copper loop

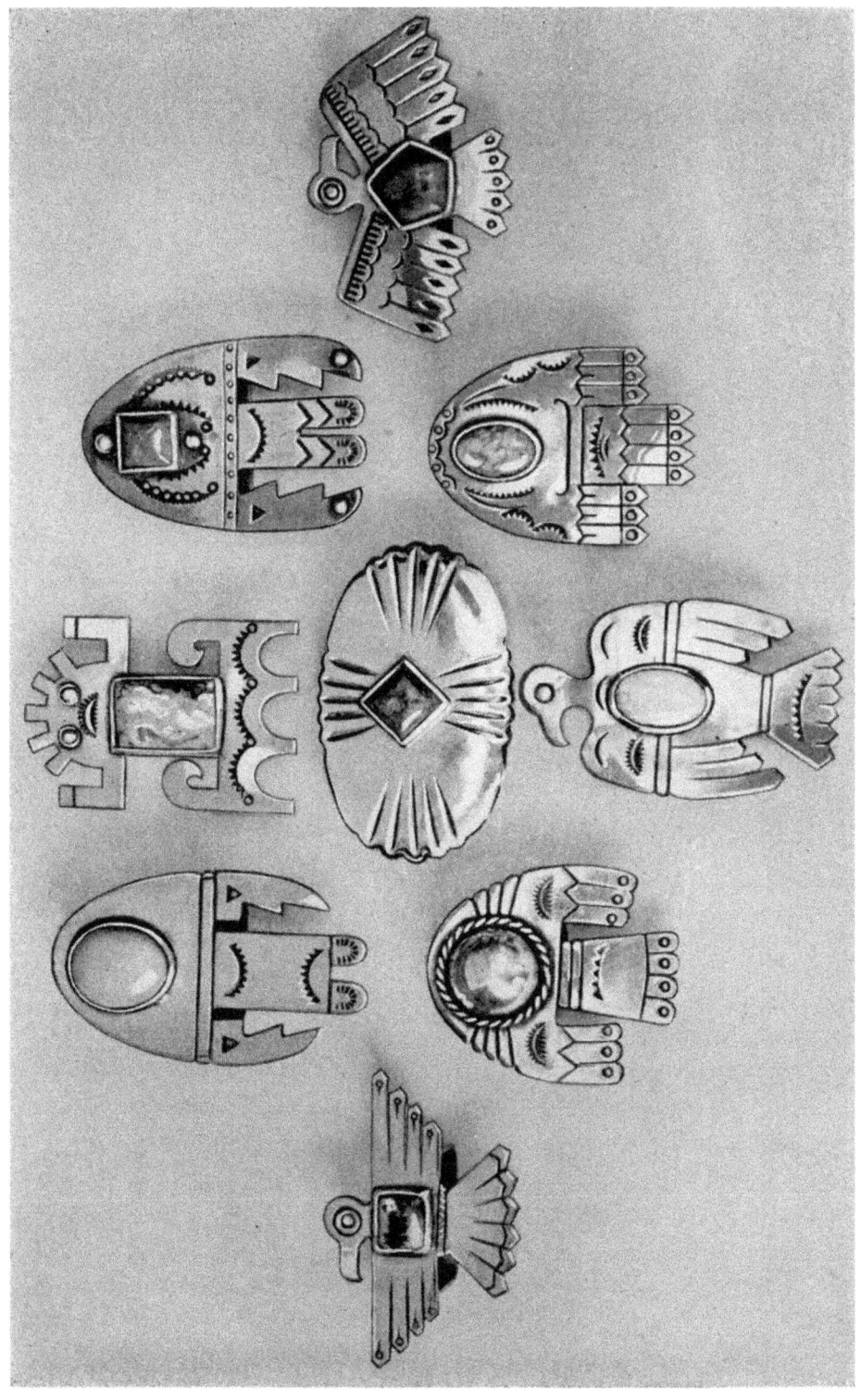

FIG. 33. Additional designs for silver neckerchief slides with an Indian motif

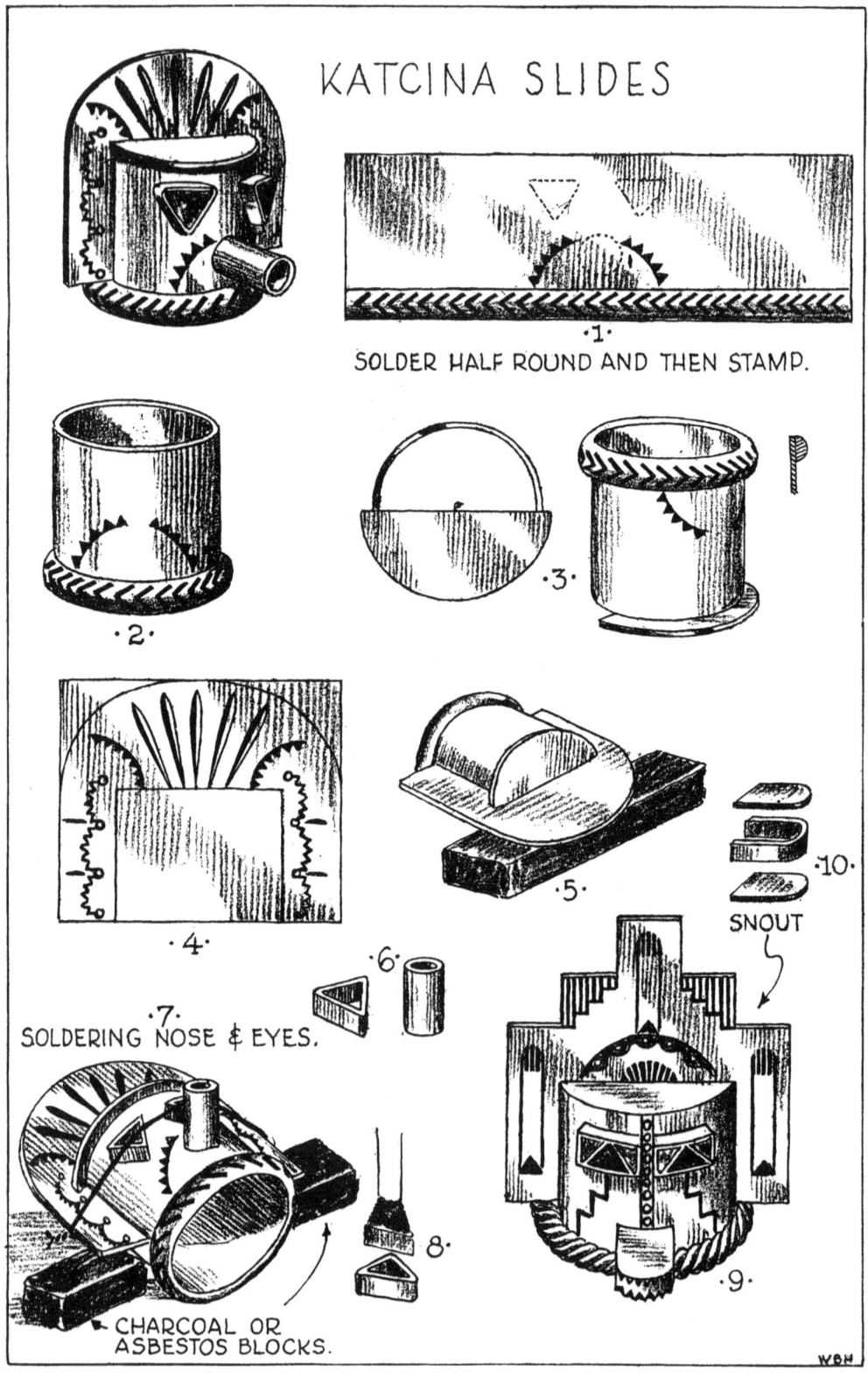

PLATE 25

Katcina Neckerchief Slides

NECKERCHIEF slides like these are collector's items. They are not found on sale at trading posts. The ones described here are replicas of masks worn by Hopi katcina dancers.

There are about six soldering operations on each one. Medium and easy-flowing solder may be used for attaching the separate pieces although the one shown and described was soldered entirely with easy-flowing solder. Rouge was painted over the first soldering joints to prevent any possible melting. The step-by-step instructions shown in Plate 25 tell the story pretty well, and are as follows: Solder the half-round wire to the blank for the cylindrical piece, 1, Plate 25, and stamp it and the other designs before bending it. Also stamp Number 4 before cutting it to shape to insure a good snug fit for soldering to the cylinder. Solder the eyes and nose first and then file the bases to fit the mask. Wire the eyes in place for soldering, but just set the nose in place and solder it.

Attach the turquoise for the eyes to lap sticks, as shown in Number 8, to grind them to fit the bezels. They should fit very snug and should be set in cement. Then grind the surface level with the bezel and flatten the edges of the bezel slightly with a burnisher.

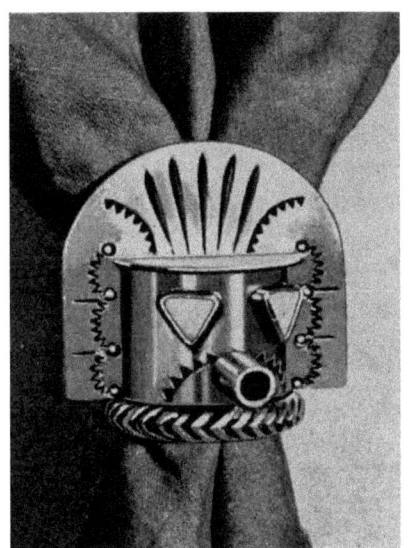

FIG. 33A. Katcina slide

In making the slide shown in 9, Plate 25, use twisted wire for the ruff and solder it to the cylinder after it has been bent to shape. Build the snout of three pieces, as shown at Number 10. The eyes are a little more difficult since they should be set with turquoise and jet. For the jet a piece of phonograph record may be substituted.

These neckerchief slides are not as difficult to make as they appear at first

BOX-TOP DESIGNS

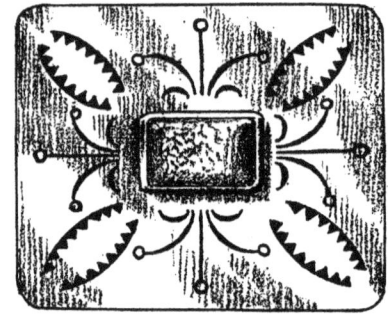

STAMPED COVERS

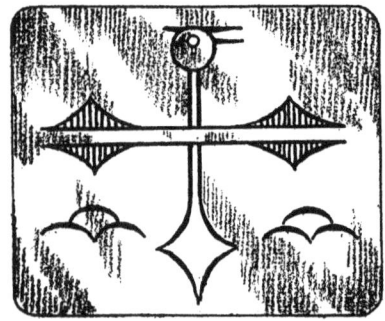

APPLIQUED DESIGNS

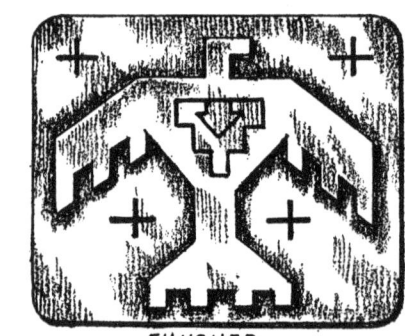

FINISHED — BLANK SAWED OUT

SOLDER SNIPPETS IN PLACE

TURQUOISE AND APPLIQUED TOP →

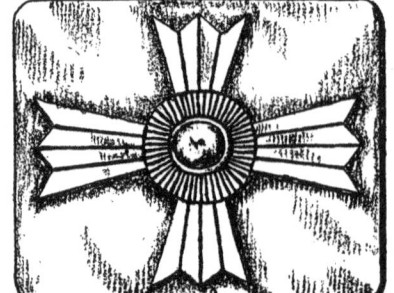

PLATE 26

glance, and if the parts are carefully filed and fitted, the soldering is more intriguing than difficult. There are a great many more designs of katcina masks that may be adapted to these slides.

Interesting lapel pins also can be made by leaving off the back half of the cylinder, and letting the flat ornament, shown at 4, Plate 25, cover the entire back.

Appliqué Work

QUITE frequently Indians use appliquéd ornaments on their silver jewelry when they have no turquoise. These appliquéd ornaments can be made quite attractive with an added stamped design or with a piece of turquoise.

In preparing an ornament that is to be appliquéd, first draw the design. From this, make a template and trace the design onto a piece of 20-ga. silver with sharp scriber. Then stamp it and solder on the bezel if one is required. Next, saw out the ornament as shown in Plate 26 with a fine jeweler's saw, and smooth the edges with a file. Place this ornament in position, and scribe a fine line around it to show where it is to be soldered. Apply flux to the piece to which it is to be appliquéd, and place snippets of solder along the *inside* of the scribed outline, as shown in Plate 26. Flux the bottom of the ornament, and place it in position. Then lay the two pieces on a soldering screen because the heat should be applied to both pieces equally. As a rule, if the two pieces fit together fairly well, the weight of the upper piece will be sufficient to produce a good sweating job. At times, however, it will be necessary to apply a light pressure to force the two pieces together so that a good soldering job may be obtained. Of course, if both pieces that are to be soldered together are very light, pressure must be applied immediately.

Another method of sweating two pieces together is to flux one side of the smaller piece, place the solder snippets upon it, and then heat it just enough to melt the solder. Then, after fluxing it, place it in position on the other piece and apply the heat until the two pieces have been properly sweated together.

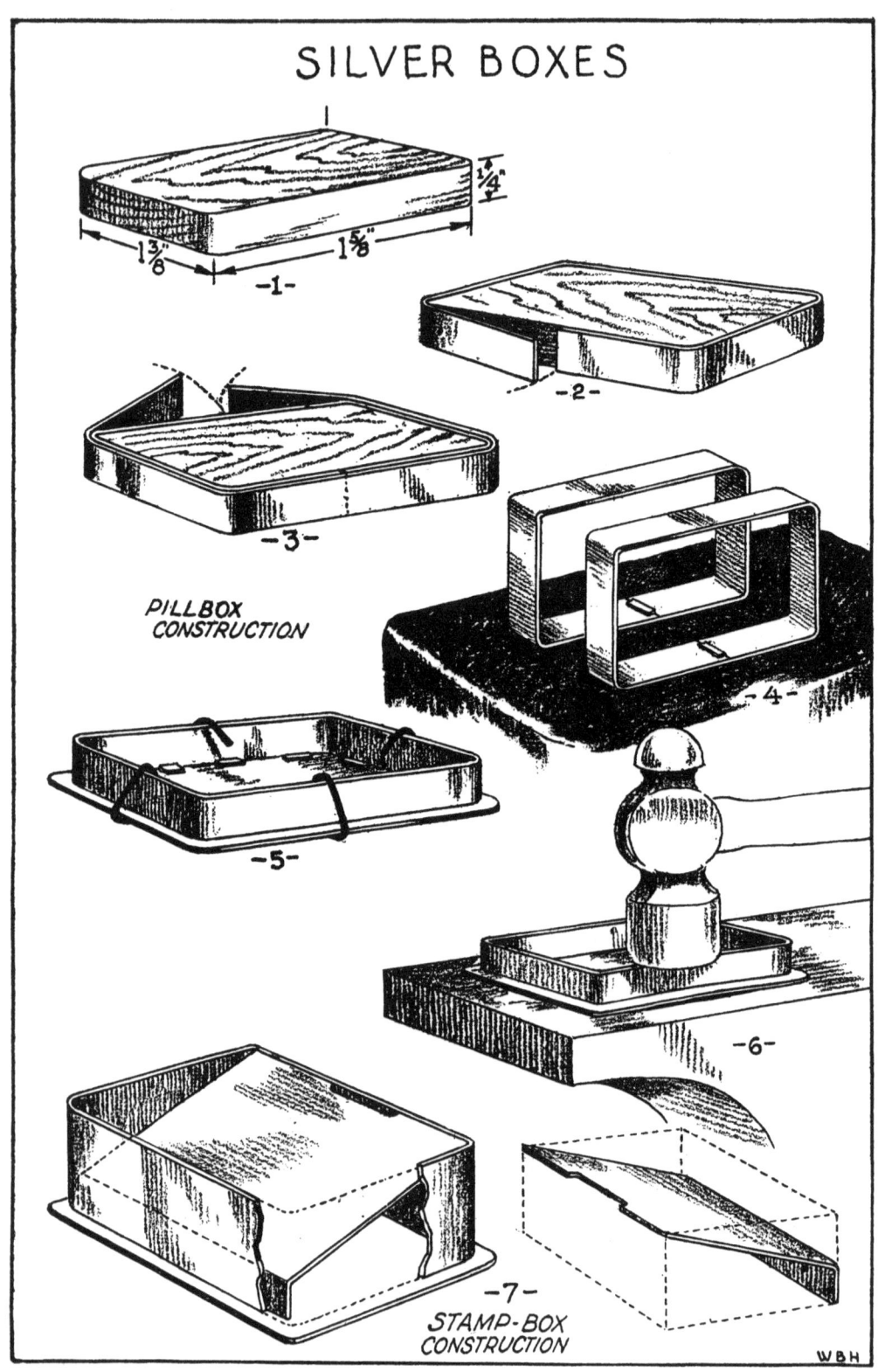

PLATE 27

Pill and Stamp Boxes

AMONG the articles made by modern Indian silversmiths are various types of boxes. Some are so small that they can be used only as pillboxes or for postage stamps, while others are large enough to serve as cigarette cases or for other similar purposes.

The small boxes can be made of 24-ga. silver. The simplest way to construct them is in two parts, the one fitting over the other, without hinges.

Steps 1 through 6, Plate 27, show how to make a box. First, cut and shape a piece of wood the size of the inside of the box. Around the outside of this form, wrap a strip of 24-ga. silver, and cut it so the two ends make a flush butt joint as shown in step 2. Shape a second strip of silver around the first strip and cut off the ends so they, too, make a snug butt joint as shown in step 3.

Step 4 shows the setup for soldering. If the pieces have been bent to shape carefully, no wiring will be required for soldering. Use a medium solder and, after it has cooled, dress down the solder at the joints and check the fit between box and cover. The two should fit snugly with just a little friction. If they fit too tightly, file the inner band slightly, or stretch the silver in the outer band by hammering lightly along the sides to be stretched.

When the bands have been properly fitted, make the top and bottom

FIG. 34. Silver pill box

of the box. Cut these two pieces so that they project ⅛ in. beyond each of the sides.

Ornament the top of the box cover with one of the designs in Plate 26, or make a new design.

The cover must, of course, be stamped before it is soldered to the sides. Due to the stamping, cutting, or annealing, the top and bottom pieces quite frequently are slightly warped. If they cannot be flattened out to fit tightly to the sides, wire them as shown at 5, Plate 27, across from side to side and bent over the sides. Use an easy-flowing solder for this last soldering operation.

Next, cut the edges of the top and bottom pieces so that they project evenly. A slight amount of warp due to the tight wiring or to slightly uneven surfaces, may be corrected as shown at 6, Plate 27. Be sure to tap very lightly with the hammer.

At 7, Plate 27, is shown a stamp box. These boxes usually are made ⅝ or ¾ in. high. The slant insert should have a small cutout at the upper edge so that the insert can be removed. The lower part of this box is large enough to hold quite a number of stamps, while the top will hold a smaller number for immediate use.

The cover of a box as deep as the stamp box may be made as deep as the box itself, or it may be made to come down ¼ in. over the sides.

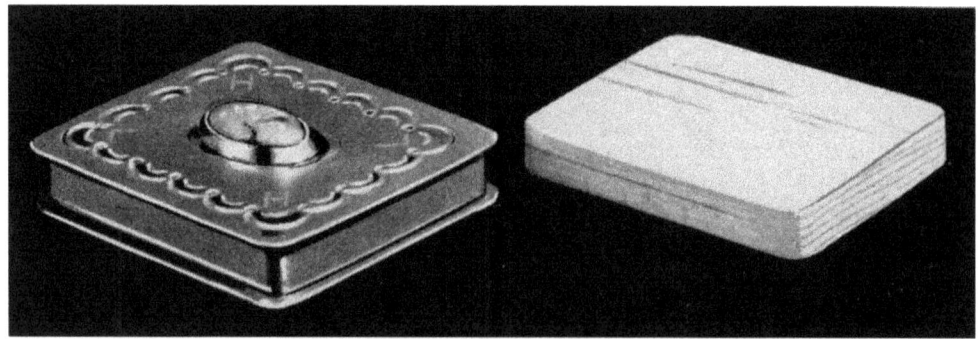

FIG. 35. Small silver box and wood form used to shape it

Oval and Round Saltcellars

ANOTHER article in silver that Indians are making is the saltcellar. This most likely is due to the foresight of some trader who saw sales possibilities in them for the tourist trade. Some pretty saltcellars seen in trading posts of the southwest are shown in Plate 28. The oval design is the prettiest, but also the most difficult. To make this, a die made of maple or birch end-grain wood must be used. Lay out the oval and, with a gouge or crooked knife, carve out a depression to the dimensions desired. Make the top and bottom pieces in the same die by hammering 24-ga. silver down into the die with a ball-peen hammer. After dapping out the two halves, file them to fit snugly. Then lay out the part to be cut out of the top piece, and saw it out with a jeweler's saw. Next, file it to an even surface so that the twisted wire rim will fit on it.

First, solder the top and bottom together and file the joint smooth. Then attach the bottom rim, the twisted wire edge, and the handle. The handle can be dispensed with if desired.

If only one grade of solder is used, paint the first soldered joint with rouge to prevent the remelting of the solder when successive soldering jobs are put on. The upper part of the saltcellar may be decorated with jiggle engraving.

The other two saltcellars shown are made in the same way as the one just described. Any stamped decoration must, of course, be put on before the respective bands are soldered.

The spoons are simply handles soldered to dapped-out half spheres.

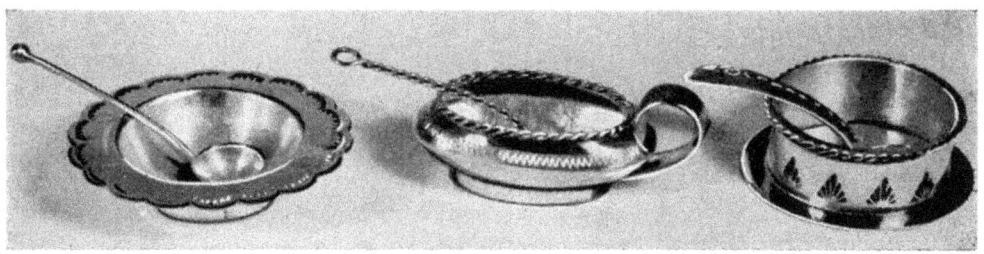

FIG. 36. Saltcellars and spoons. Made by the author after Indian designs

PLATE 28

Bracelets of Sheet Silver

THE bracelets described herein represent work that is larger and more complicated than most of the projects described before. They can be made as delicate as fancy rings or they may be made as big as the massive bracelets seen in the southwest, where men wear them as well as women. Figures 37 and 38 and Plate 29 present quite a variety to choose from. The bracelet at the top in Figure 37 was made by a Zuni silversmith. The small, deep blue turquoise, which adorn it, show it to be typically Zuni. Zuni work usually is set with many small stones. The small stones are easily and quickly ground and polished and are not as expensive as the larger ones.

The second bracelet in Figure 1 also was made by an Indian silversmith. The base of the third bracelet is made of square wire. This bracelet was made by a Navaho. The stones are very fine but crudely cut and polished, and the bracelet is simple to make.

Number 4 in Figure 37 was made by the author. The triangular wire, used as the base, was hammered to that shape from round wire in a V groove filed in a piece of rail. All of the pieces were soldered together at one time as shown in Plate 29.

Number 5 in Figure 37 presents the problem of soldering the half-round strip to the edge of the band. The straight lines are stamped in first. The half rounds are soldered at the same time as the bezels.

The soldering must be carefully done because the bezels are of very thin metal and the half rounds are quite heavy. Therefore, in soldering, special attention must be given to the bezels, so that they do not melt. These large bracelets are best soldered on a screen frame so that the heat can be applied from top, bottom, and edges. The stones are set after the bracelet has been bent to shape, polished, burnished, and high-lighted. Sometimes the solder will not melt and flow properly the first time. By working fast, these unsoldered places may be quickly coated with flux, a few snippets of solder placed where needed, and then the heat applied with care to finish the entire soldering job. It also is possible that, after

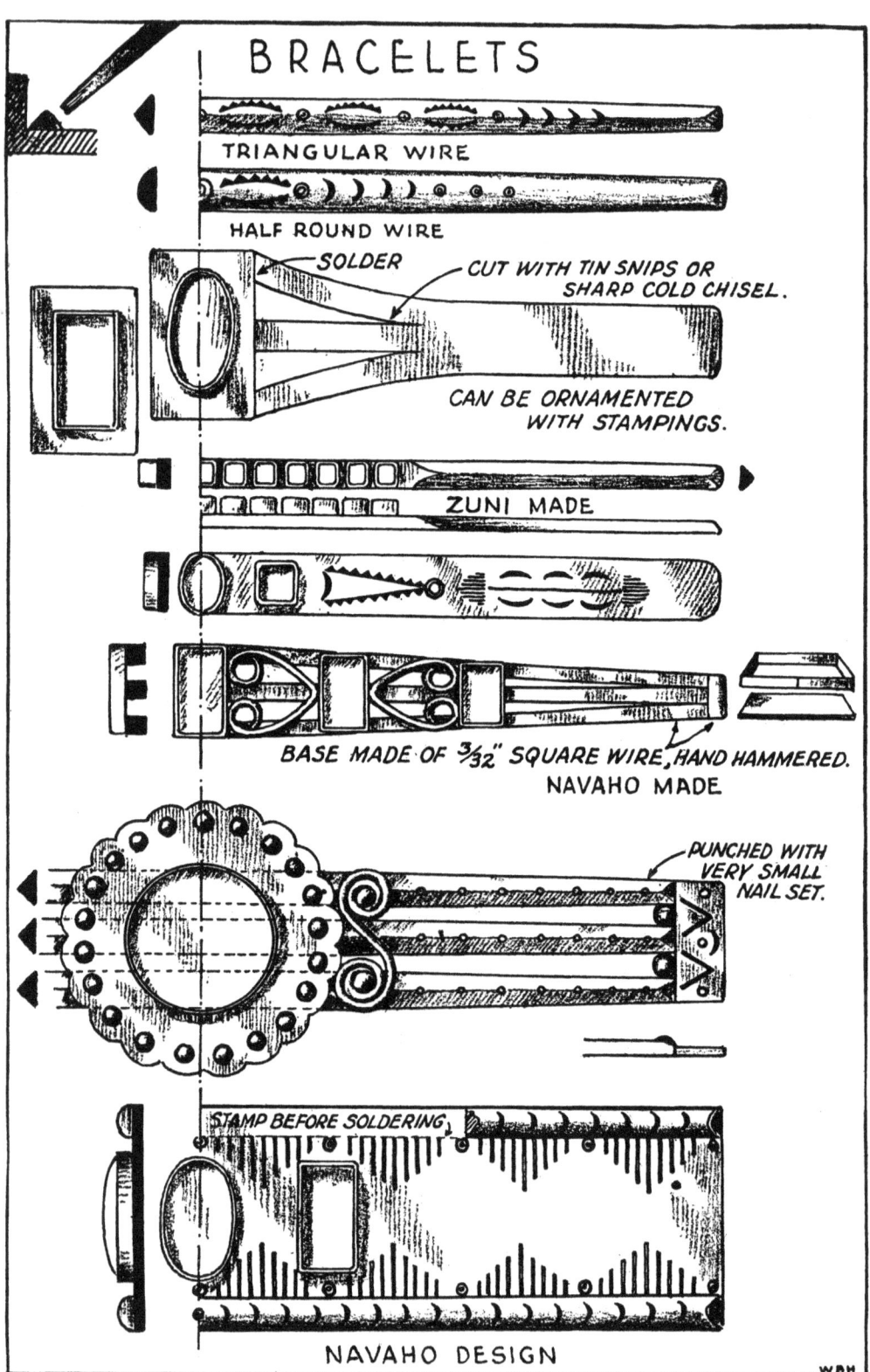

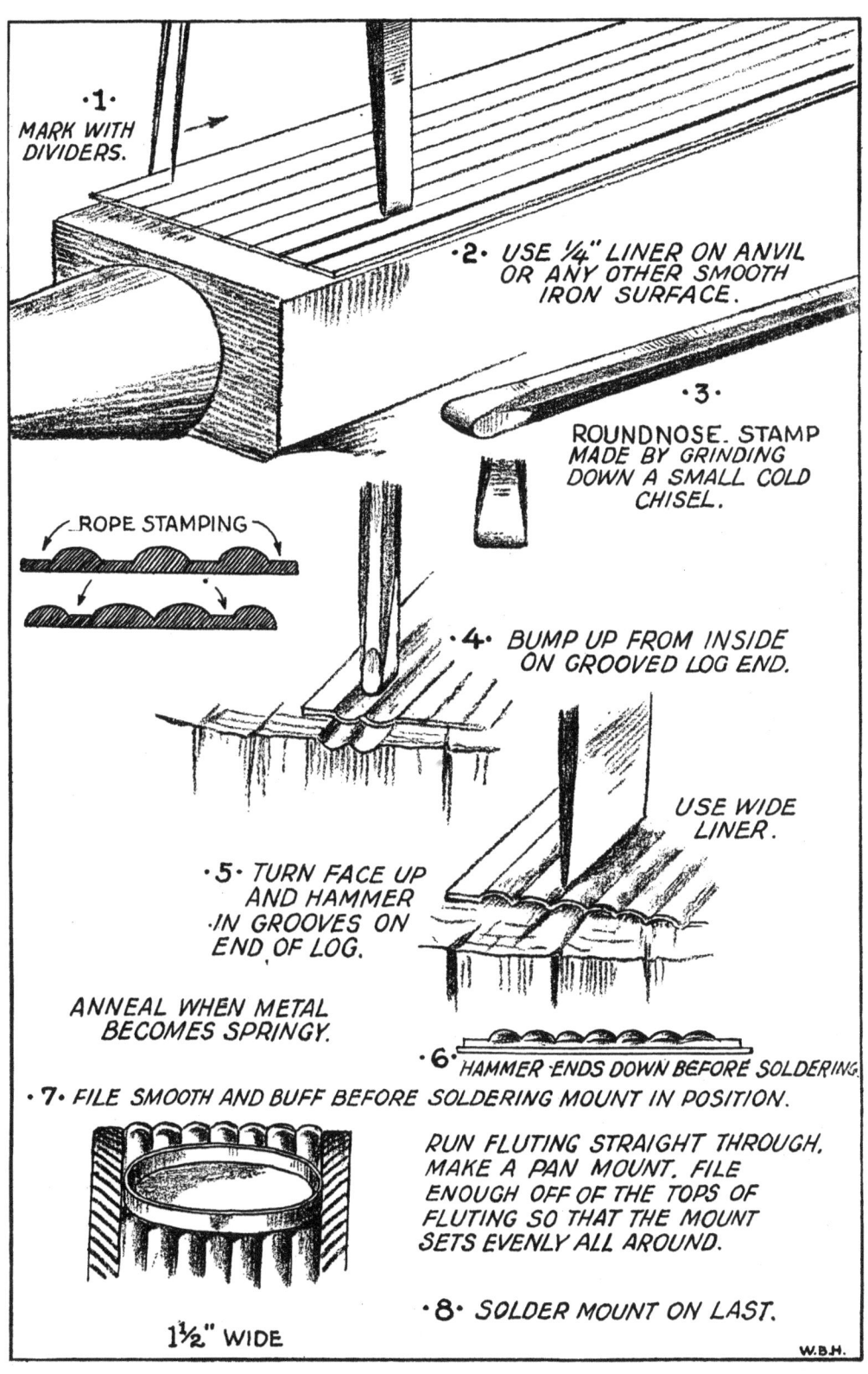

PLATE 30

FIG. 37. Bracelets of various designs

FIG. 38. A beautiful example

the bracelet has been cleaned up in the pickle bath, flaws will be found in the soldering. In that case, wash it carefully and thoroughly in clean water, dry it, and then put flux and solder on and finish up.

The sixth bracelet in Figure 37 is a typical Navaho design, and is beautiful without the turquoise setting, which was added by the author. The Navahos usually make these bracelets of very thick metal, and apply a variety of flutings and stampings, mostly of the rope pattern. Indians form the bracelets by hammering and filing, but this is a laborious job. Plate 30 shows the several steps in making such a bracelet. Use 18-ga. silver for the face, and proceed as follows:

Lay the blank on a smooth piece of metal or glass, let one point of heavy dividers ride alongside the edge of the silver, and scratch in parallel lines, as shown in 1, Plate 30.

Follow these scratched lines with a ¼-in. lining tool as in step 2.

Make the roundnose stamp shown at 3 to be used for bumping up the fluting. This can be made quickly out of a small cold chisel which will need no extra tempering.

Next, cut two shallow grooves in the end of a log or a block of hardwood. These grooves may be cut in with a handsaw, and should be the same distance apart as the lines scratched into the silver. With the roundnose stamp made in step 3, round out a groove between the two grooves cut with the handsaw. Then turn the metal face down, as shown in step 4, and hammer or bump up the ridges. Use a fairly heavy hammer for this as it saves time.

The grooves will look rather bumpy at first, but after they have been

FIG. 39. Tapping down bezel with light wooden mallet and square-faced tool

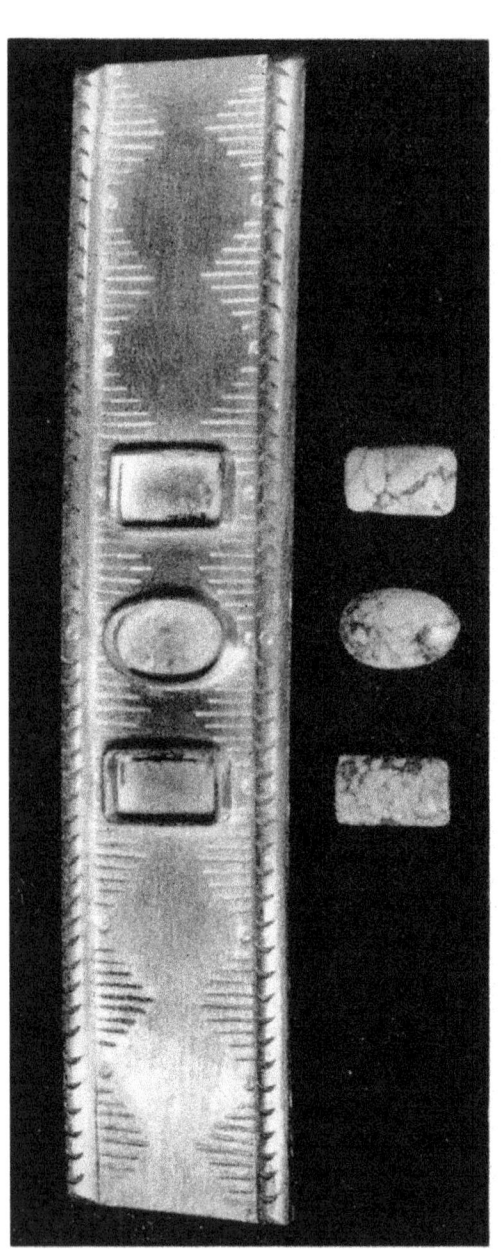 

FIG. 40. Blank cleaned with pickle and powdered pumice — ready for buffing

formed, turn the blank over and, with a wide lining tool, pound down the lines, using the end of a log or hardwood block to pound on, as shown in step 5. Repeat this process until the blank looks fairly even, and then anneal it.

After the blank has been annealed, tap it flat with a rawhide or leather-faced mallet. Then bend it in a shallow arc until the center is about ½ in. higher than the ends. Next, with a small triangular file, remove the small bumps in the groove. Then, with a flat file with a fine cut, file until the fluting is even. Flatten out the blank again, and stamp the edge. The blank is ready for soldering on the back. The bracelet would look too thin to be made of one thickness of metal, and the back or inside of the bracelet would be rough and unfinished, but the author has seen them made that way.

To make the back, cut a piece of 18- or 20-ga. silver the same size as the face, and anneal it if it is springy. See that both face and back fit together snugly even if a bit of filing on the bottom of the fluted piece has to be done. Hammer the ends down to a close fit before soldering. There are two methods of soldering. One is to place the solder snippets between the two pieces, wire the pieces together, and solder. The other is to cut the lower piece about $\frac{1}{16}$ in. larger all around and place the solder snippets on this projecting edge. The latter method may be found the simpler. Put flux along the edges of both pieces for a width of about ¼ in., and wire the pieces spirally along the entire length, with soft iron wire. Place the solder snippets along the projecting lower piece after the wiring is on. Then place the whole thing on a screen soldering frame and apply the heat. The author also has used split cotter pins as clamps along edges to be soldered, with good results. Play the flame over and under the entire piece, and when the solder melts, follow it along the edges. Wherever it does not flow right, place on more flux and solder and continue heating. When the entire job has been cleaned, buff and shape the bracelet.

Shape or form the bracelet before the stones are set, especially when large stones are used, because the stones may break in the bending process.

Bend bracelets over the horn of an anvil or a rounded piece of hardwood held in a vise. When large stones are used, leave the top of the bracelet flat for an inch or more so as not to bend the setting. Bending will not alter small settings such as those shown in all but the fourth and sixth bracelets in Figure 37, but to play safe, set the stones after forming.

Figure 39 shows how stones can be set, by using a square or oblong-faced punch, and tapping lightly with a small wooden mallet while the piece is clamped in a vise. Pieces of blotter or leather are placed on either side of the bracelet to prevent the jaws of the vise from marring the edges.

The lower bracelet in Figure 40 shows another bracelet that can be made of 18-ga. silver. This bracelet was made to match a ring, the setting of which was identical to the setting on the bracelet, though somewhat smaller. Figure 40 shows this bracelet in the flat, and to exact size so a drawing is unnecessary.

Plate 31 shows sketches of Indian bracelets seen by the author while traveling through the southwest. Anyone interested in Indian silversmithing can make similar sketches of desired pieces. Even though the sketches may be rough and may not carry every detail, the worker can trust his memory when trying to make his own designs.

In Plate 31, only one half of a design is shown in the sketch. This saves time, yet presents all that is required when both sides of a bracelet are identical.

Number 1, Plate 31, shows a two-piece bracelet; that is, the mount or setting is soldered to the bracelet proper. Number 2 also has the setting soldered to the bracelet. The outer bands on this and the one shown in number 5 are of twisted wire, hammered carefully to about one half of the thickness of the original twisted wire. Number 3 is quite an intriguing design. All the stones are solid blue with no matrix, and the only attempt at ornamentation is the row of raindrops around the large stone. Number 5, while rather overelaborate as far as design goes, is very attractive with its setting of petrified wood in yellow, orange, black, and purple. Numbers 4 and 6 speak for themselves, while 7 needs a little explaining. It is built up on a flat band, and the half rounds and the setting, which extends to the arrow-shaped points, are soldered on.

Bracelets of Hammered Silver

SOME traders and some of the national parks will not accept Indian jewelry that has been made of sheet silver. They prefer to buy articles made of silver that has been hammered out. On the reservations, away from cities and before rolling mills were so universally available, all silver was melted, cast into ingots, and then hammered out to the proportions and sizes needed for the particular piece to be made. This procedure involves more work than using sheet silver, but the results are much more gratifying.

Molds can be cut out of a brick or can be made of plaster of Paris or of graphite or any other material that will withstand heat. For the bracelet shown in the upper part of Plate 32, the ingot was about ¼ by ½ by 3 in. The mold was heated and the silver was poured into it until it was level with the top. When making ingots, do not let the silver get too hard, so that it cannot be hammered out. To anneal silver, heat the piece to a red heat. When it blackens, grasp the ingot at one end with common pliers with serrated jaws, and hammer the flat side, changing ends from time to time until the piece has been hammered out evenly. Then set it on edge on the anvil, and hammer the edges with a fairly heavy hammer. Do not hammer silver too long, as it becomes hard and brittle rather quickly and will fracture or crack. To prevent this, anneal the silver frequently. It will seem slow work at first, but gradually the piece will lengthen and spread. Pounding on the edges will lengthen it quickly and at the same time tend to keep it even along the full length. By the time it has been drawn to a full 6 in., it will be approximately ⅛ in. thick or less. Now, with a rather coarse file, work it down to an even surface with smooth edges. Take out all the hammer marks. Anneal it again, and mark it for the lining. With a scriber, scratch it fairly deep. These deep scratches will form guides for the lining chisel. With a small liner go over all the lines, then sharpen a larger chisel as shown, and go over the grooves to make them deeper, but don't cut through. To make filing easier, anneal the silver again and bend it as shown in Figure 41. Now, with

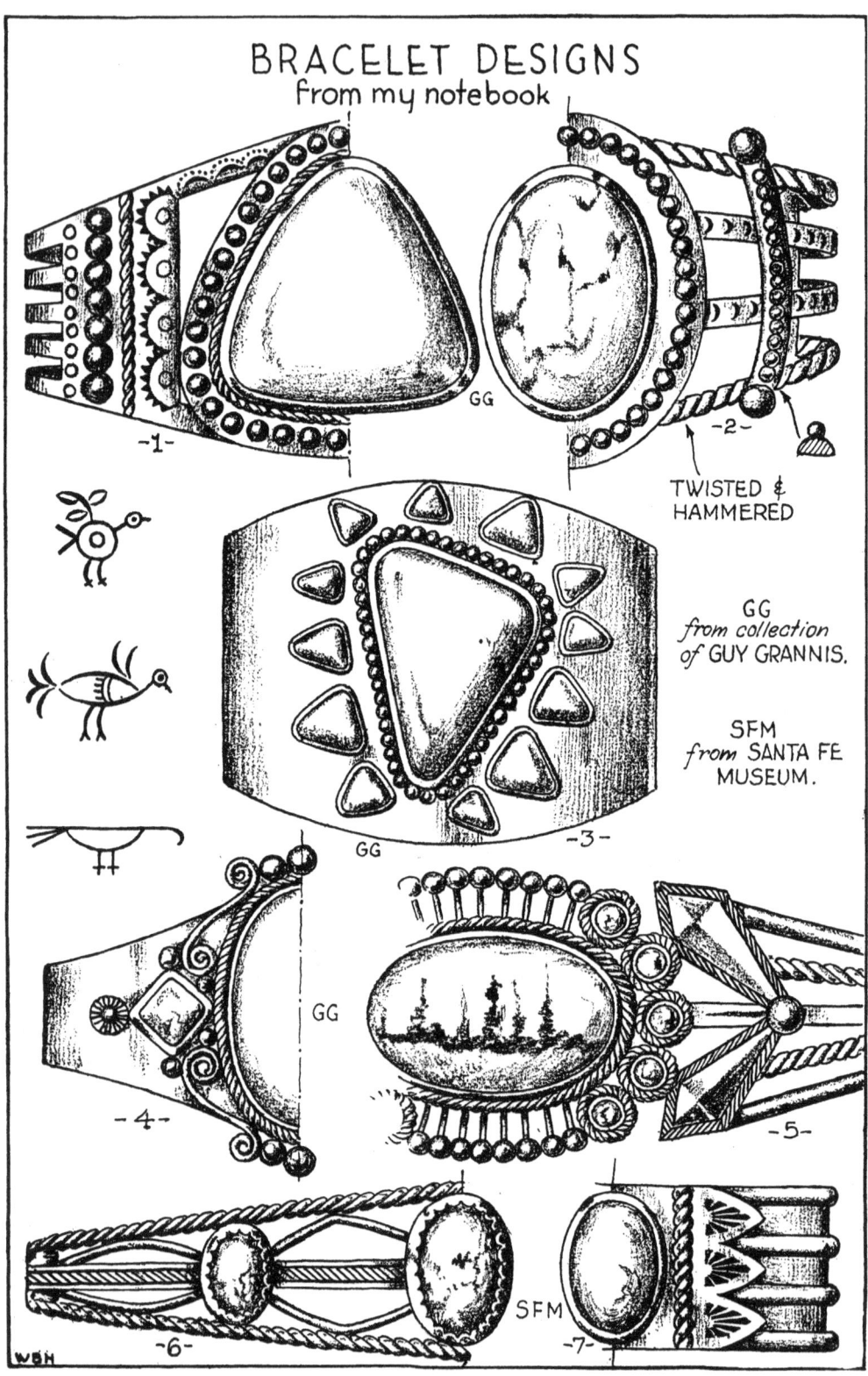

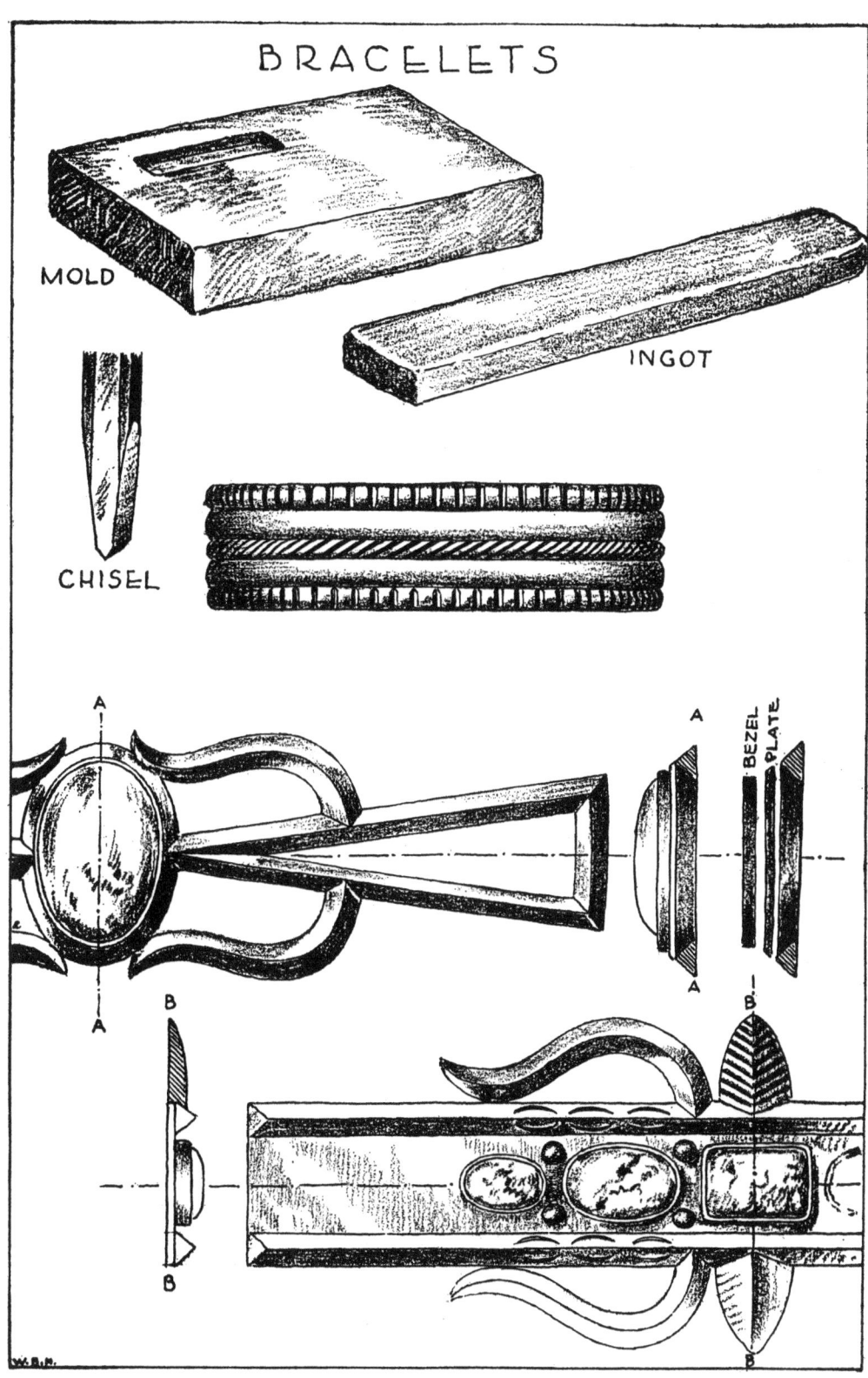

PLATE 32

either a triangular or a mill file, round off the edges to make nicely rounded fluting, and finish with a finer file. Straighten out the blank again to do the stamping on the edges and the centerpiece. Use the large chisel for the two sides and a small liner to do the rope stamping. Now curve the piece again, and file it to remove the burrs that pushed up in stamping. Then polish and shape the bracelet to fit the wrist.

The two bracelets in the lower half of Plate 32 are imitations of cast bracelets. The author drew both designs. The lower one is the more attractive and easier to make. Since the author had only a large stone, he could not make the lower bracelet which requires several smaller stones. He, therefore, made the more difficult of the two bracelets. The triangular wire in this case was hammered out of heavy square silver wire, in the V grooves of a piece of rail iron. It could be hammered out of heavy round wire just as easily, or it could be purchased ready made. After hammering the wire, it must be filed to a uniform size. About 20 in. of triangular wire is needed for this bracelet. The miters are cut with a jeweler's saw and then filed to fit snugly. If the wire is annealed, it is easily bent, as shown in Figure 2.

This bracelet is made as follows: File the points of the cow-horn pieces to shape, and bend the wire before it is cut off the long piece of stock. This makes the operation of shaping easier. Hold the wire with a pliers with rough jaws, after a piece of leather has been placed over the jaws to prevent marring the silver. The rough jaws keep the leather from slipping.

Do all soldering on a smooth charcoal block. Lay the pieces together for soldering. First, solder the large triangles shown in Figure 42, with medium solder. Then solder the total assembly shown in Figure 42, and file off the surplus solder. Now cut a plate for the base of the bezel housing, and file it to fit the oval. The best way to handle the housing is to solder the bezel onto the base plate with medium solder. Then solder the plate

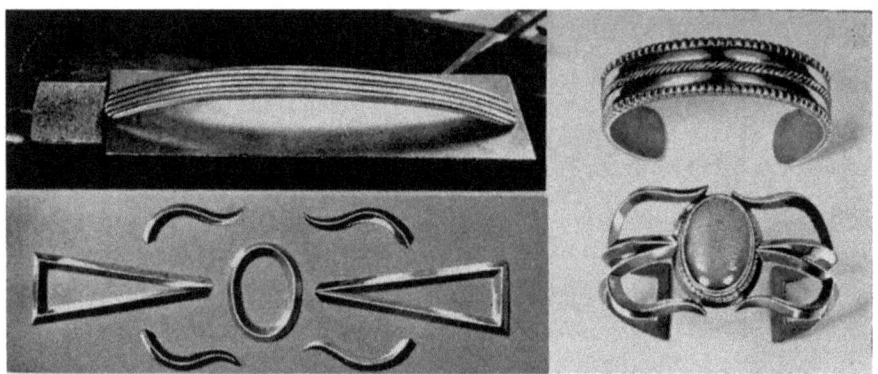

FIG. 41. Upper left: Blank bent to make filing easier
FIG. 42. Lower left: Parts assembled for soldering
FIG. 43. Right: Finished bracelets

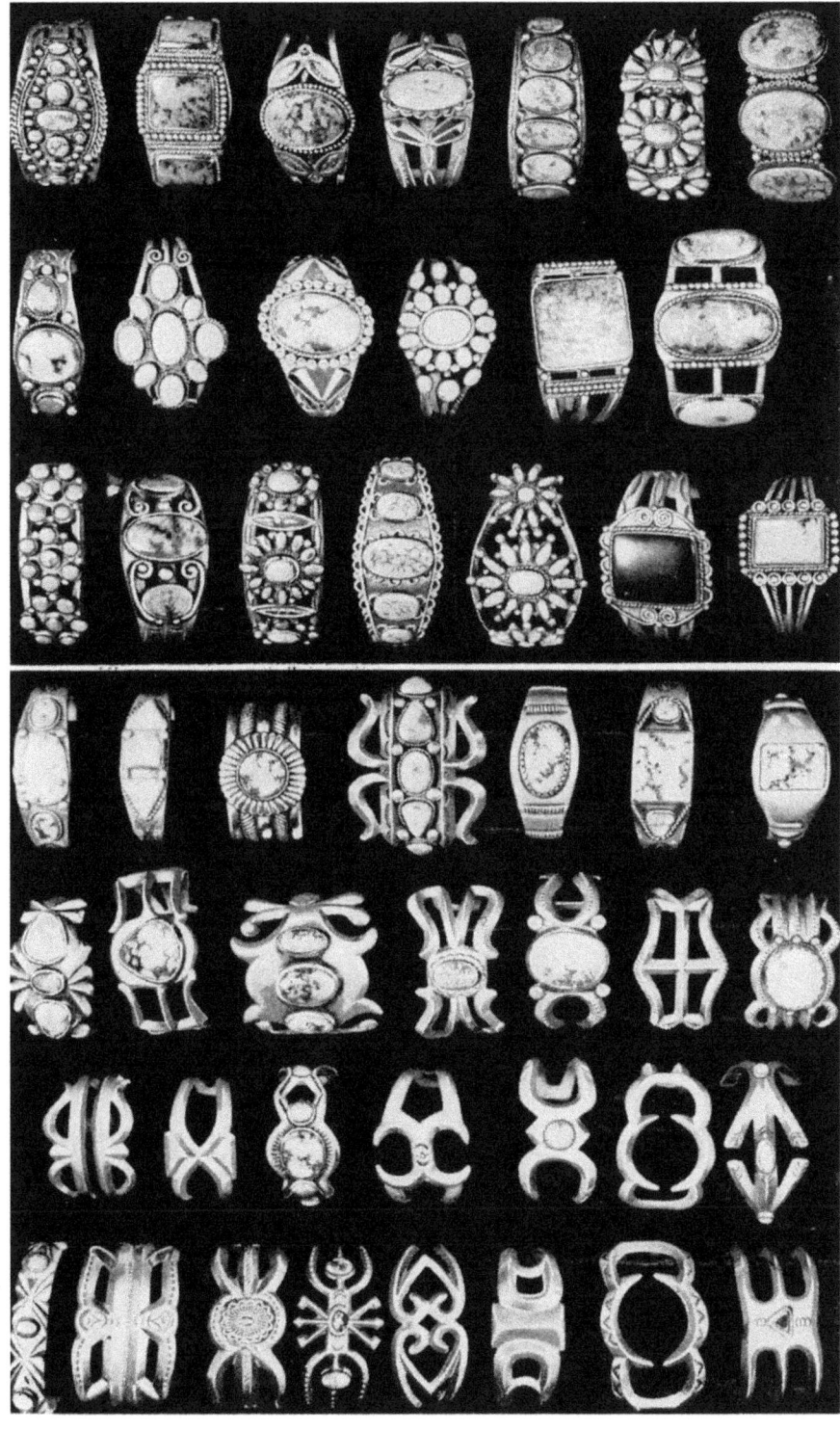

FIG. 44. Cast Indian-made bracelets from the collection of Buck Burshears, La Junta, Colo.

onto the triangular wire oval with easy-flowing solder. Do the stamping around the bezel on the base plate with a very small nail set.

Care must be taken in shaping the bracelet to the wrist. Bend it over a round piece of hardwood, and be sure to bend the cow-horn sections to correspond with the long pieces. Quite a bit of bending can be done with the hands. Set the stone last. The lower sketch shows a much prettier bracelet, but for real beauty it needs five matched stones in the settings shown. Both of these are tricky to make but they are well worth the effort.

Figure 44 shows two sets of Indian made bracelets that may be of help to anyone desiring to create new designs.

Arm Guards or Ketos

THE arm guard, or keto, as the Navahos call it, is the next project to be described. Ketos belong to the days of the bow and arrow. They were the leather arm guard worn to protect wrist and arm when shooting with the bow and arrow. The silver keto is merely a symbolic decorative article.

D, Plate 34, is a wide leather band that can be worn with one of the silver ketos shown. At E, a silver keto is held on with two leather straps. Ketos of this kind are now used as bracelets which are quite frequently worn by Indian men. The two narrow straps are much cooler to wear than the wide leather band, which formerly was the actual bow guard.

The ketos in Plate 34 were sketched with the permission of the Santa Fe Museum. Many of those shown at this museum were of cast silver. The ones shown at A and B in Plate 34 are of wrought silver, and the one at C is a wrought design adapted from a sketch made from a cast-silver keto on exhibition at the museum. Invariably the wrought ketos have a half-round wire soldered around the outer edge. This not only adds strength to the thin sheet of silver, but gives a more substantial appearance to the finished article.

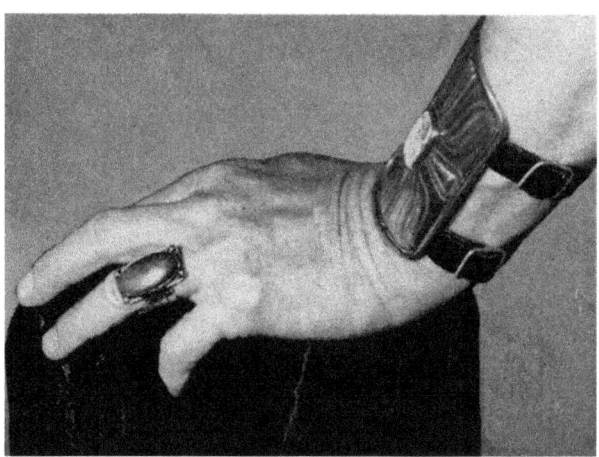

FIG. 45. Showing how the keto is curved to fit the wrist

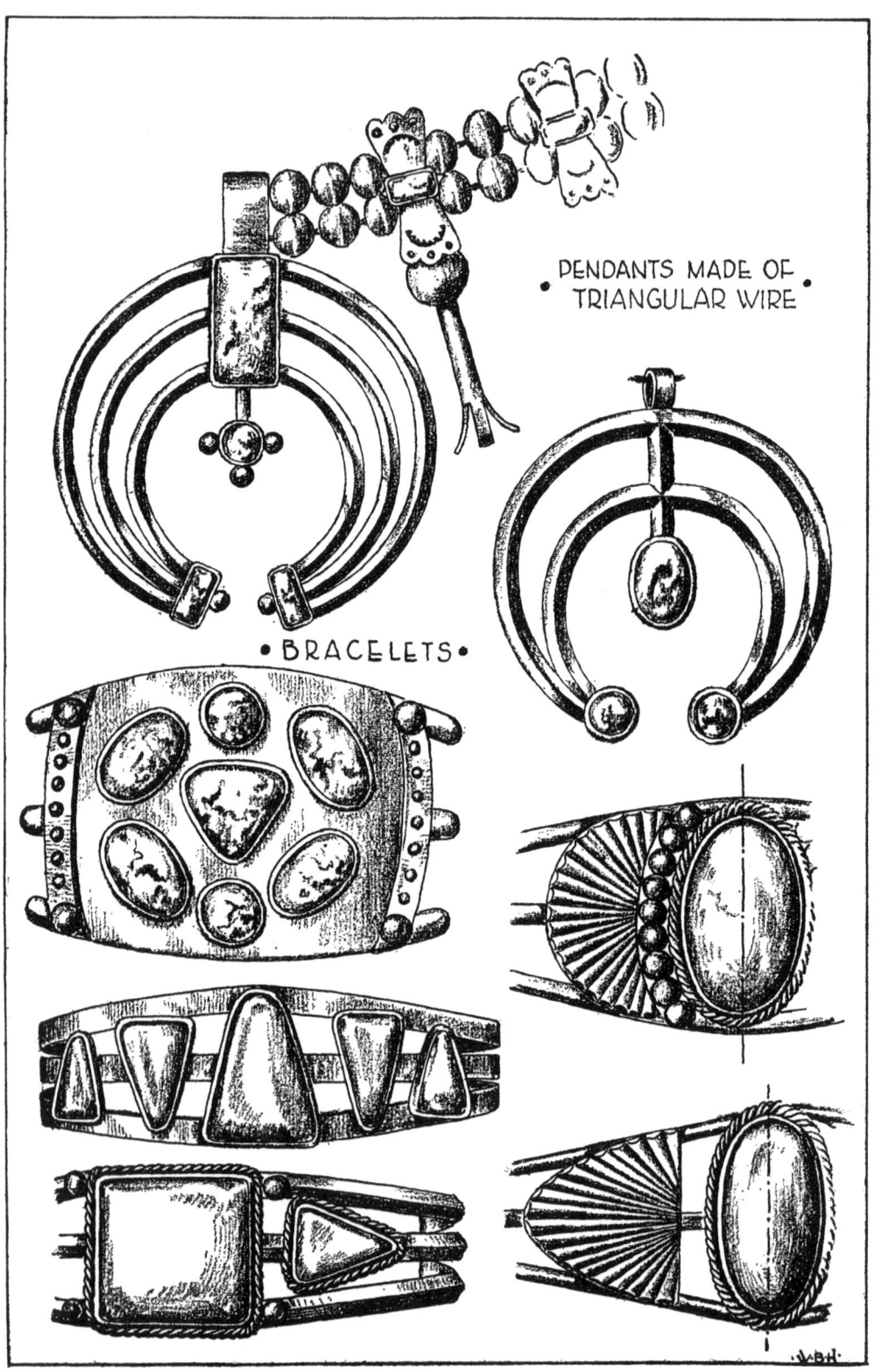

PLATE 33

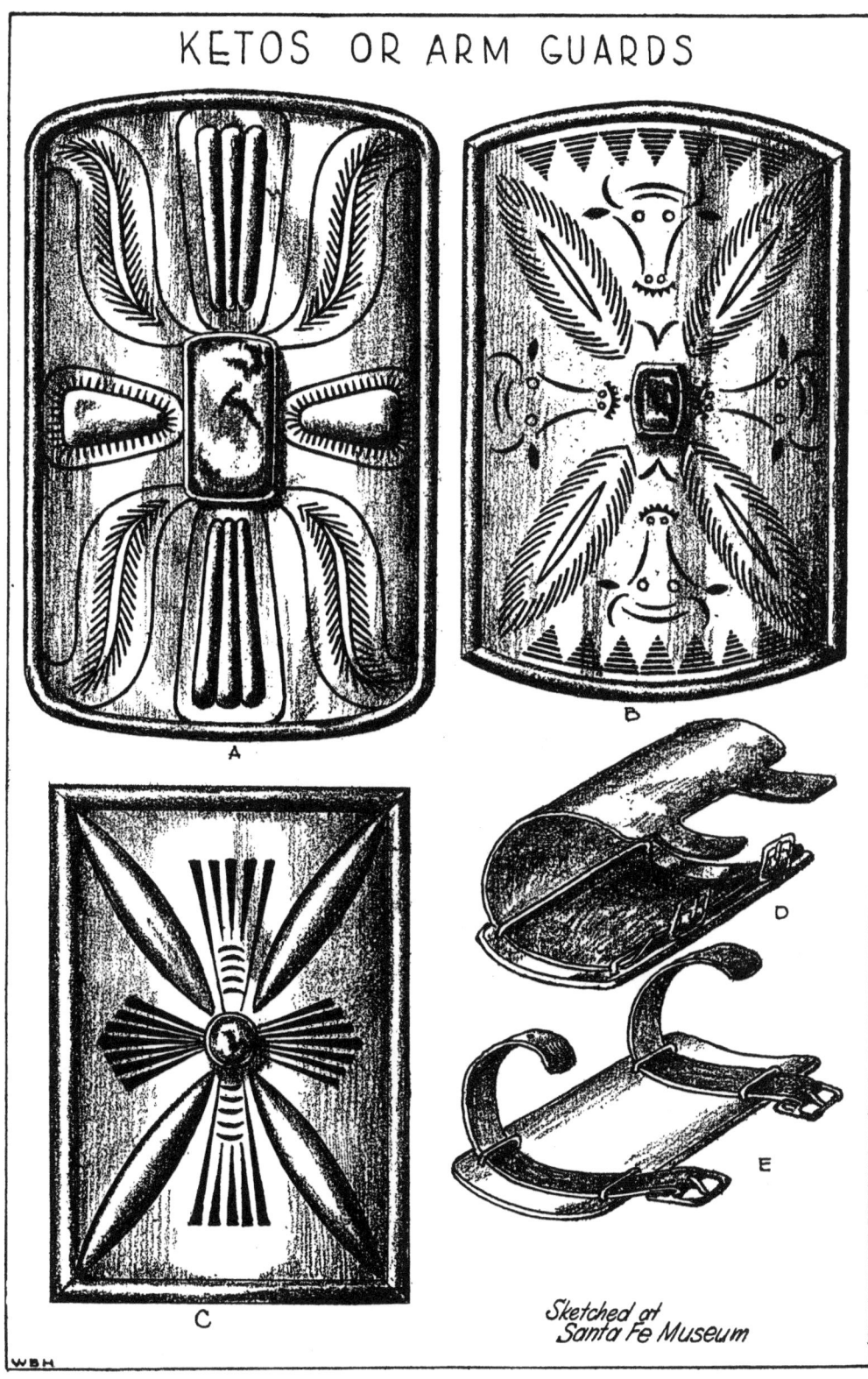

PLATE 34

To make the keto shown at A, trace the entire design. Then transfer this design to a piece of 20-ga. silver, using typewriter carbon paper. Next, transfer the same design with carbon paper, to the end of a hardwood log, or trace it on the end grain of a hardwood block. With a small gouge, carve out the triple bumped-up design and the one at the side. Only one of each of these needs to be carved. Be sure to carve them in the right position, so that, when the one set has been bumped into the silver, the blank needs to be turned only halfway around for the second bumping operation.

The stamped ornamentation must, of course, be put on before any bumping is done. After the bumping has been completed, touch up the plate with a file, if necessary, and then polish to a good finish. After that has been done, solder the half-round wire around the outer edge.

If no half-round wire is at hand, make some as follows. File a round groove with a small rattail file into a block of steel, and then hammer a piece of 10-ga. wire into the groove, thus forming a half-round wire that will be quite acceptable. Move the wire along as it is hammered, and then finish it with a file to take away the irregularities.

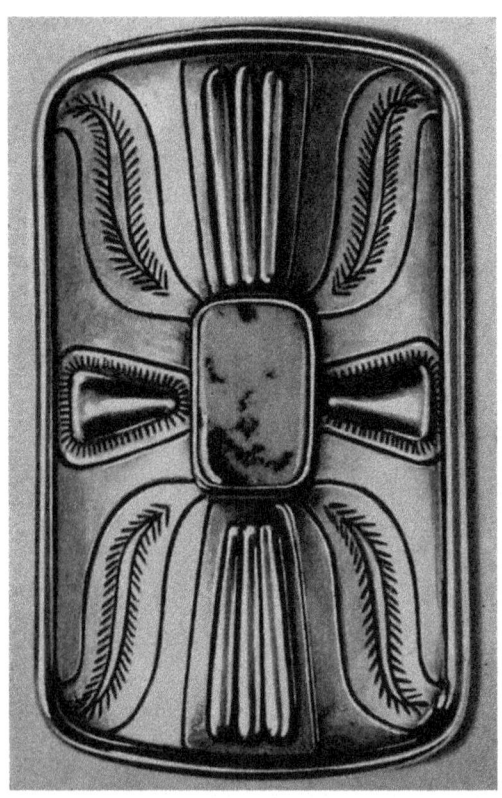

FIG. 46. Silver keto ornamented with turquoise setting

When the soldering of the half-round wire has been completed, round the keto over a rounded piece of hardwood until it fits over the wrist and arm as shown in Figure 45.

The next step is to put on the turquoise. The stone shown in Figure 46 was shaped on a carborundum stone and then polished with fine carborundum cloth. The final finish was given to it with tin oxide and water on a piece of buckskin.

Of course, the wire loop or loops are soldered on before the stone is set. Indians use heavy flat or round copper wire for these loops.

The keto shown at *B* is quite simple to make since it requires no bumping. It could be made without the turquoise and would be equally as attractive.

The bumped-up ornamentations on the keto at *C* may be made separately and then soldered on.

If necessary, the buckles for the straps may be made of 14-ga. wire.

Belt Buckles

BELT buckles made of silver and turquoise or just plain silver always are attractive, and there is not a man, boy, or girl who would refuse to accept one. If the reader knows how to do leather tooling and carving, he can produce a very artistic belt. But, if he cannot do this work, he can buy a belt and make a buckle for it. Some belts have snaps for attaching the buckles, and on others buckles are sewed to the belt. If a belt with snaps cannot be obtained, it is a simple matter to rip the stitching, replace the old buckle, and sew up the belt again, using the same holes to do the stitching.

As shown in Plates 35 and 36, Indian-made buckles, as a rule, are quite a bit larger and more showy than the ordinary buckles found on the market, and they are made in a great variety of shapes and styles.

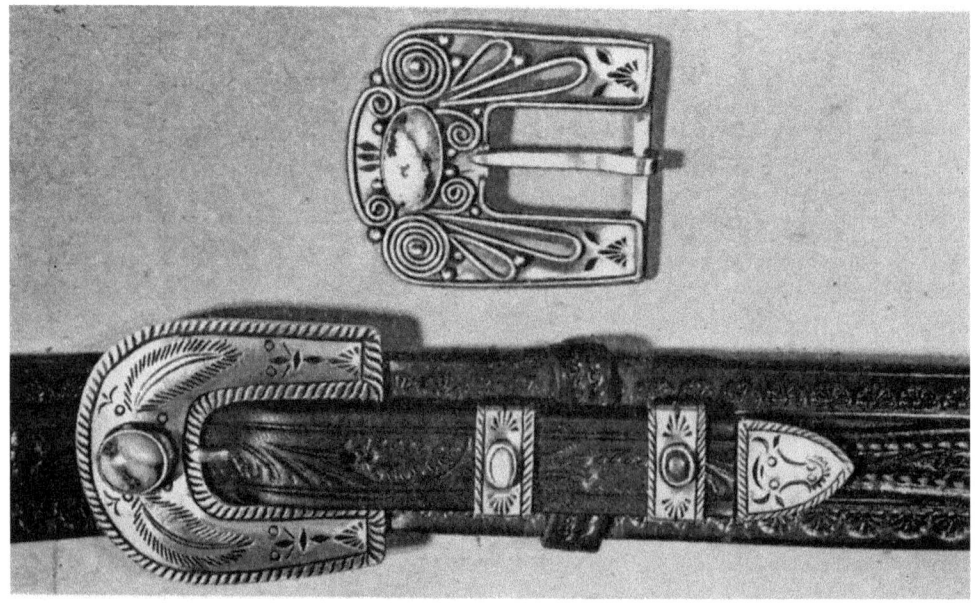

FIG. 47. Finished buckles made by author shown in Nos. 1 and 2, Plate 36

Number 1, Plate 35, is a rather plain horseshoe buckle with the bar of round wire flattened at the ends and soldered to the back. The tongues on the buckles, as a rule, are loose and have no fitted setting, but the belt holds the tongue in position.

Number 2, Plate 35, is a double-tongued ladies' buckle and was on a belt as wide as the opening of the buckle.

Number 3, Plate 35, is an elaborate buckle, and very likely was taken from a concha belt set. There are two ways in which this type of buckle can be used. By the first method, the raised ornaments are bumped up on a block of wood or on a pitch block, and by the other method, the raised sections are made separately and soldered in position, as shown in Figure 2. Jewelry made by the second method, if the edges of the ornaments are filed down to meet the base, looks very much like fine jobs of bumping up. This method seems the most satisfactory because it leaves the base or background of the piece with a smooth, even surface. Then, too, heavier-gauge silver can be used for the buckle proper when the ornaments are soldered on. A buckle should look substantial and 16- or 14-ga. silver is commonly used. If no heavy silver is available, two thinner-gauge pieces may be soldered together as described in the article on bracelets.

Number 4, Plate 35, also is a concha buckle with the outer edge flat

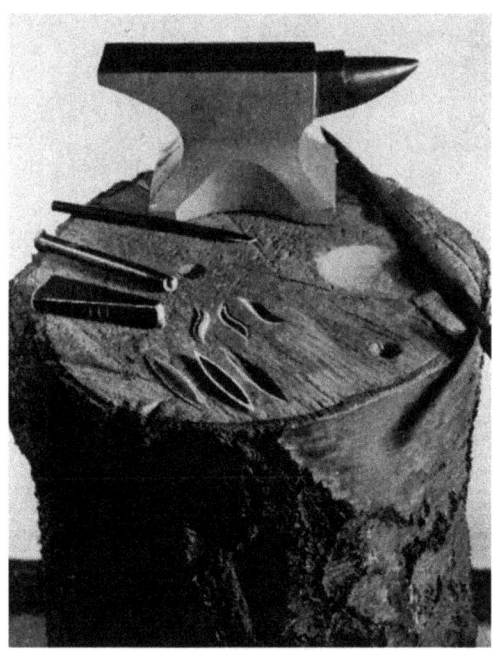

FIG. 48. Work log with depressions used to bump up ornaments for the buckle shown in No. 3, Plate 35

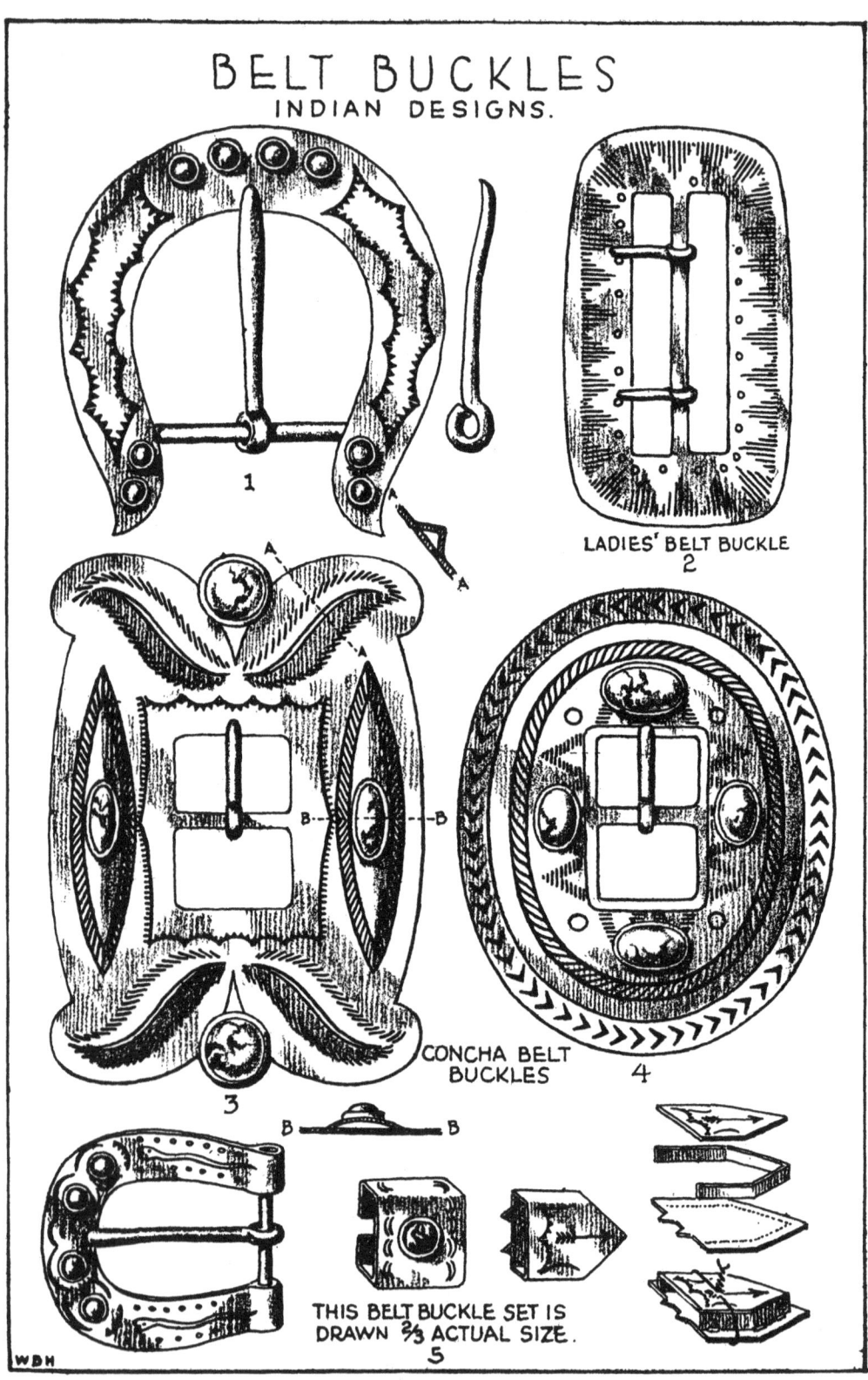

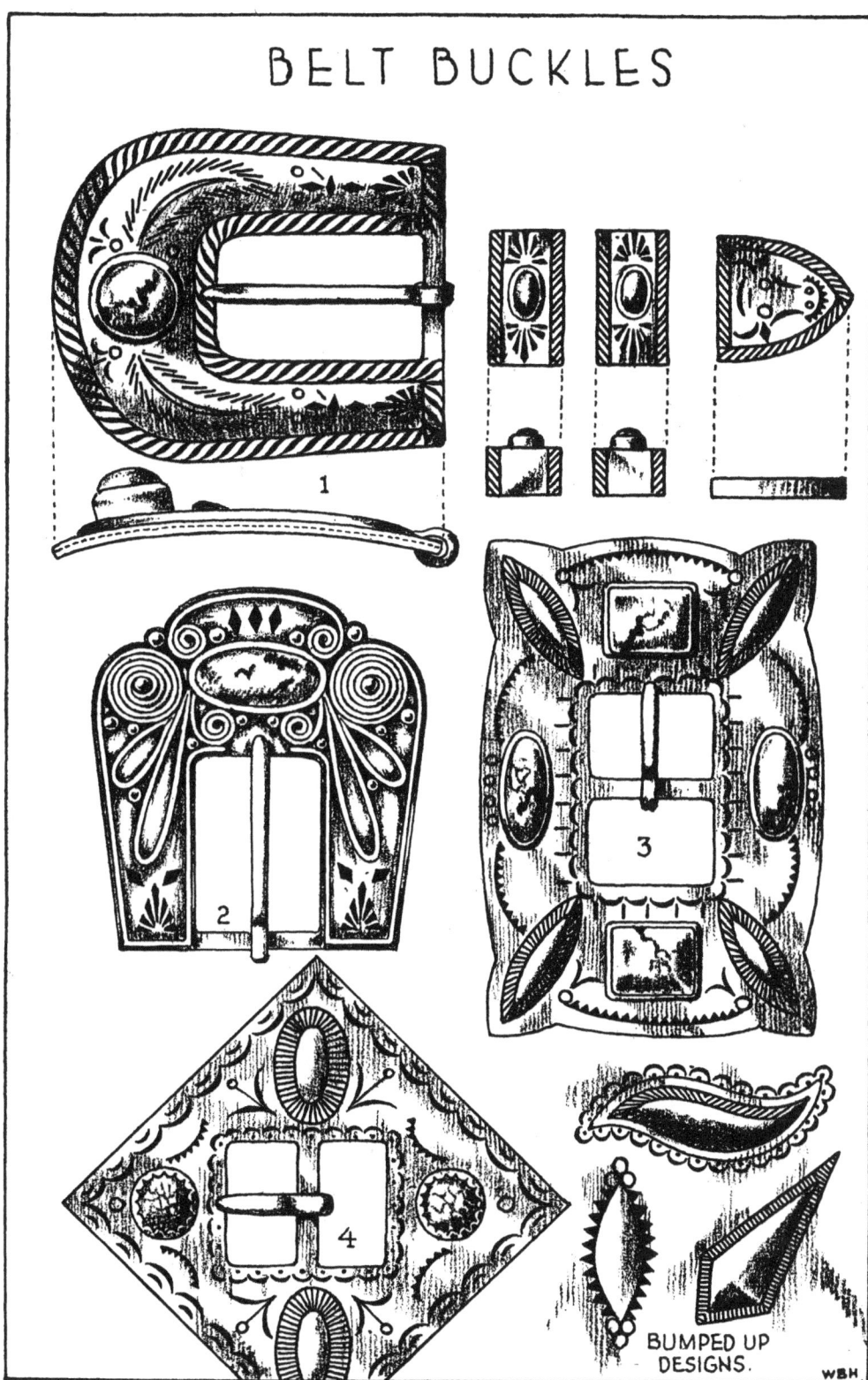

PLATE 36

and the rest slightly domed. All large buckles must be slightly curved to fit the wearer's body, otherwise the ends will project. The bending, of course, should be done before the stones are set.

Number 5, Plate 35, is a rather small buckle from a western style belt. With this buckle also are a belt loop or keeper and an endpiece. Some of these belts have two keepers as shown in Figure 47.

Plate 36 shows four buckles designed by the author. Numbers 1 and 2 are details of the buckles in Figure 47. Number 1 is made by stamping and bumping up the face and soldering a back to it. Number 2 is a rather ornate buckle of single-thickness 18-ga. silver, twisted wire, and raindrops. All the buckles shown are ornamented with turquoise.

Number 3, Plate 36, is ornamented with four turquoise, but, if necessary, the top and bottom oval stones may be replaced by raised and stamped ornaments, or as mentioned before, these ornaments may be raised and stamped, and then soldered on. The square buckle in Number 4 is a style quite often used on concha belts, but this buckle looks equally well on a leather belt. In the lower right-hand corner are three raised ornaments which can be used on large buckles. Frequently, turquoise have been mounted on Indian belt buckles where no actual space was allowed for such ornamentation. Number 3, Plate 35, looks as though the stones were added later, and buckle 4, Plate 35, shows plainly that the stones were set over old stampings. The Navahos are demanding more turquoise in their jewelry of late years, and are adding to old pieces whenever they can.

In the lower right-hand corner of Plate 35, the soldering procedure for the endpiece is shown. First, solder the sidepiece to the top in the same way that a bezel is soldered to the base. Cut the top to the correct shape, lay it face down on the charcoal block, bend the sidepiece to shape, place

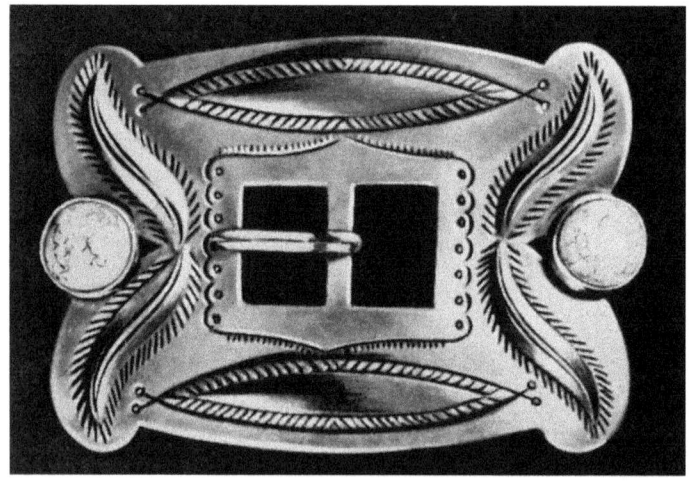

FIG. 49. Buckle similar to the one shown in 3, Plate 35. Made by author

the solder snippets inside, and solder the sidepiece to the top. Cut the back slightly larger except for the part which has the two prongs for securing it to the strap. The lower sketch shows the assembly ready for the last soldering. Cut or file and finish the edges.

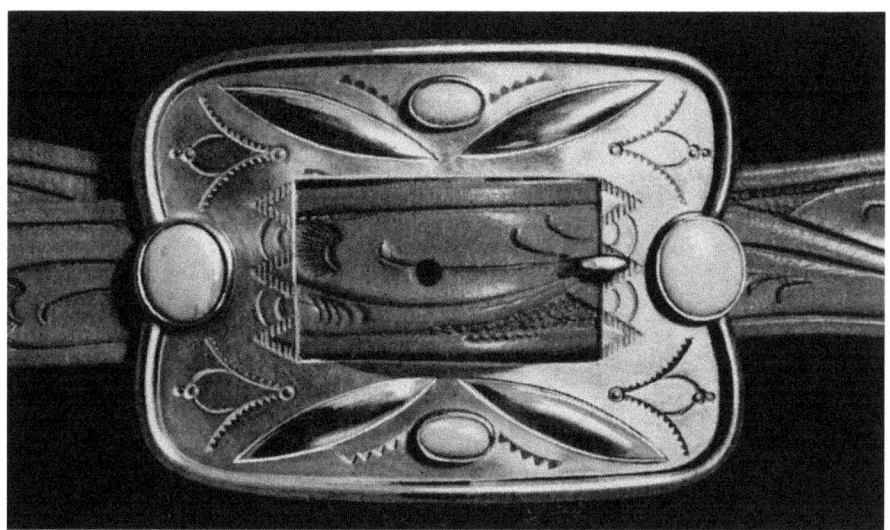

FIG. 50.   Belt buckle made by author

BELT-BUCKLE SETS

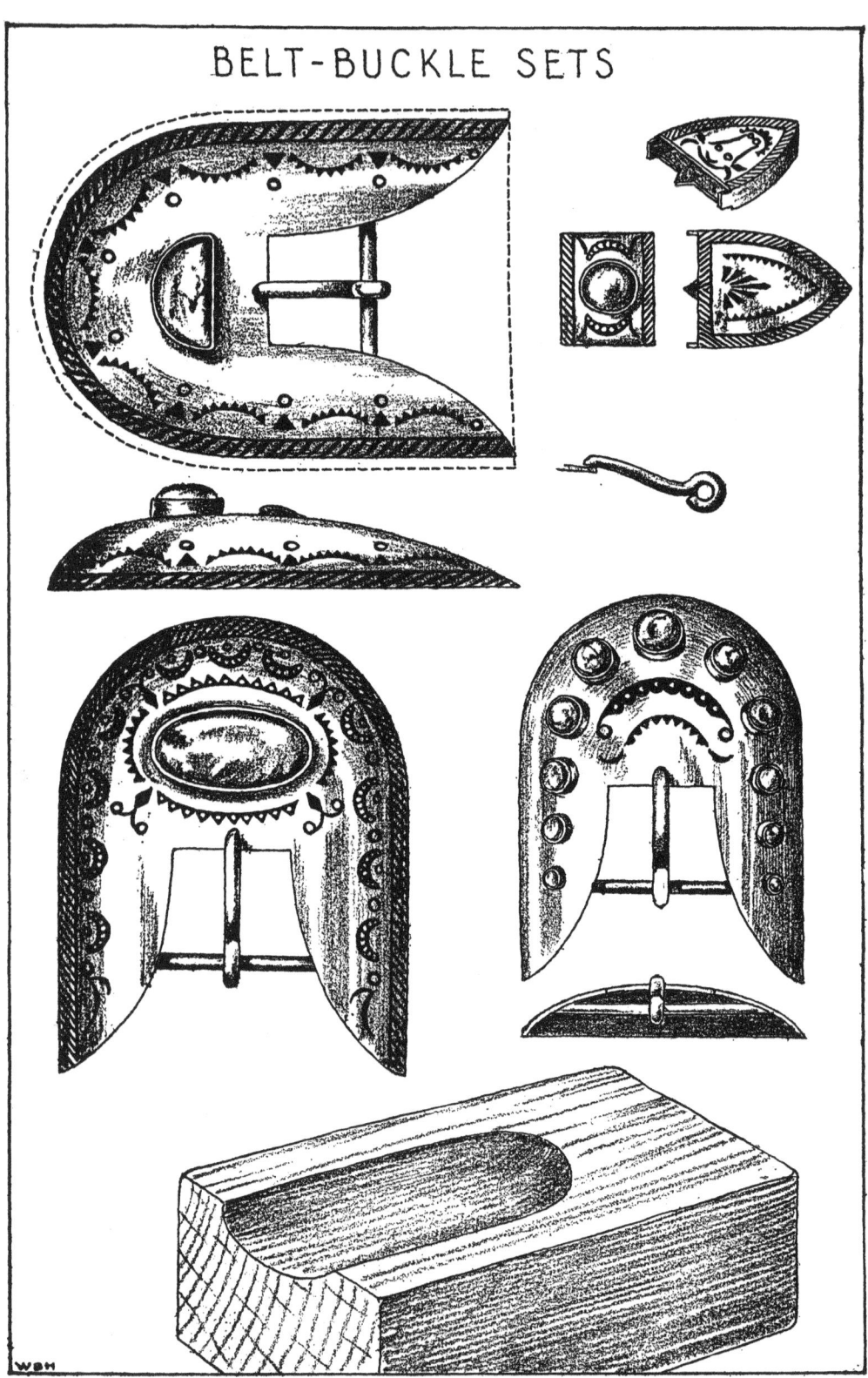

PLATE 37

Belt-Buckle Sets

THE type of buckle shown in Plate 37 appeared in the western and southwestern trading posts around 1946. To make this buckle, cut a blank as shown in the dotted lines at the top of Plate 37, and stamp the blank while it is flat. Then, with a crooked knife or a gouge, cut out a die of any hardwood, such as walnut or maple, to the shape of the finished buckle shown in Plate 37. Stamp the design and then, using a maple mallet

FIG. 51. Showing buckle stamped and ready for shaping on wood die

FIG. 52. Shaping with rounded, rawhide covered, wood mallet

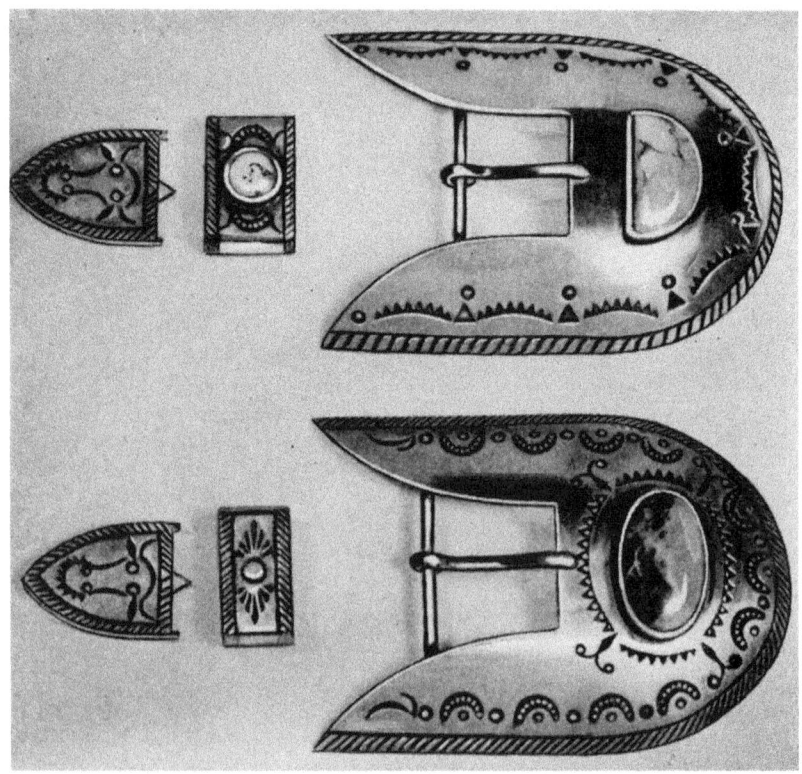

FIG. 53. Belt buckles and ends

with a rounded end covered with rawhide, shape the metal as shown in Figures 51 and 52. Any slight irregularities can be smoothed with a file. When the silver has been shaped nicely, cut out the opening with a jeweler's saw.

The half-round stone in the buckle at the top of Plate 37 was cut from a broken oval stone. When making the bezel, file it to fit the curve, and when setting the stone, cut out the center of the cardboard base usually put under the stone, to allow for the curve of the metal. Also file away some of the metal below the bezel before soldering the bezel in place.

Set the crossbar about halfway between the top and the bottom. Use any endpieces for the belt, either with or without stones as shown in Figures 53 and 54.

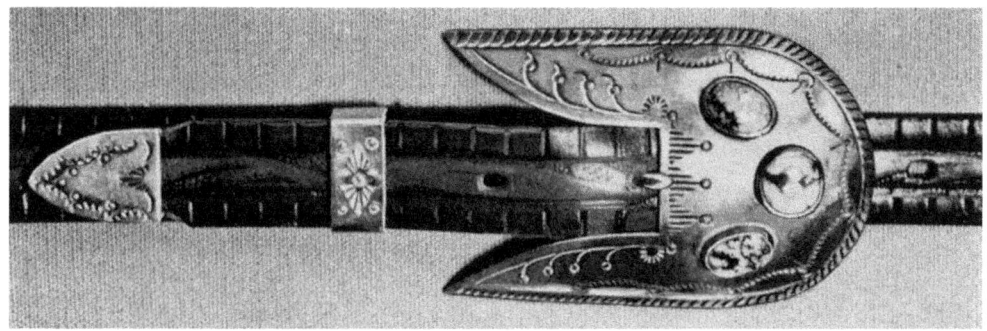

FIG. 54. Belt-buckle set similar to the one shown in Plate 37. Made by author

TEA STEEPER

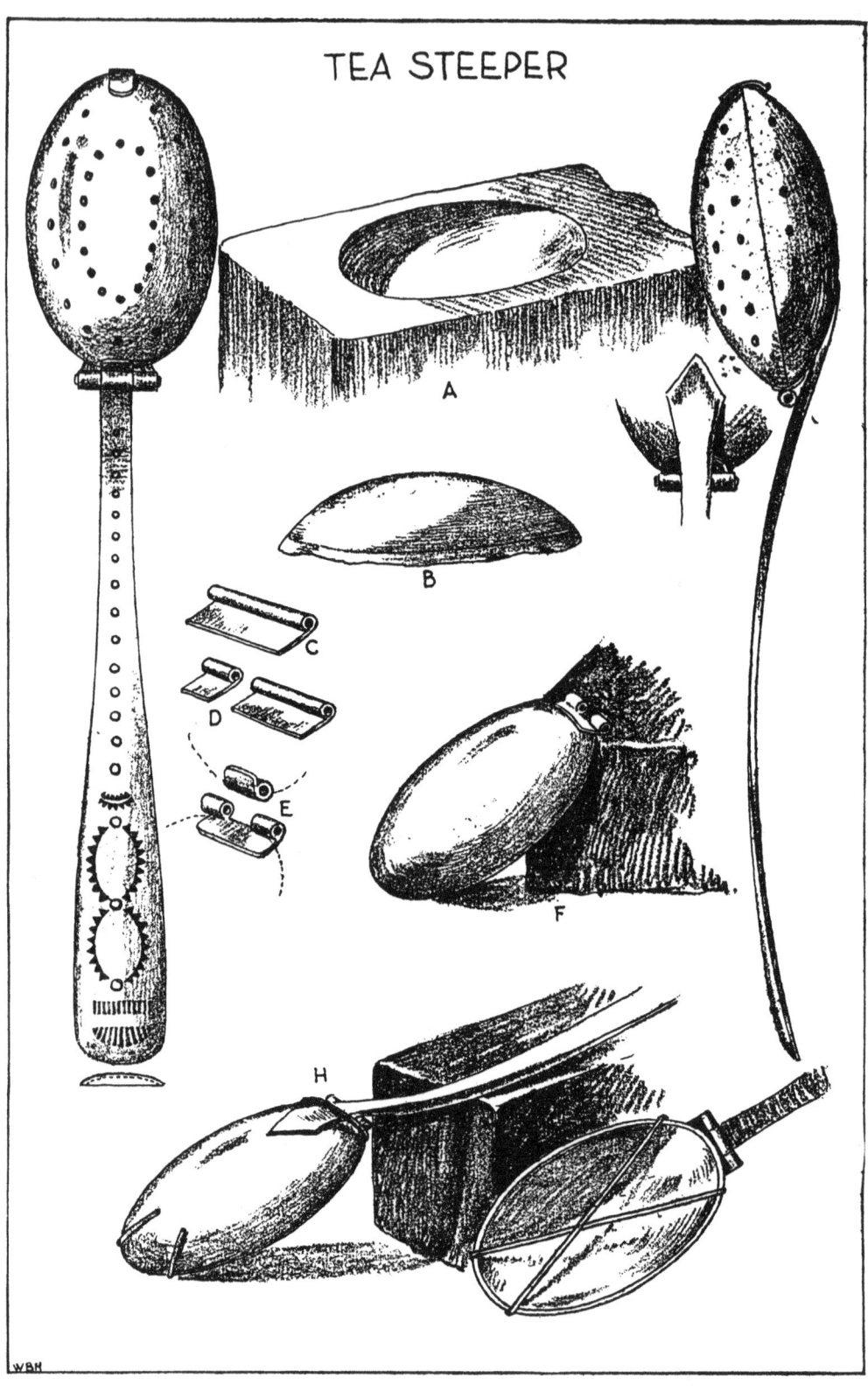

PLATE 38

Antique Tea Steeper

IT IS hardly possible that an Indian ever made a tea steeper like the one shown in Plate 38. Nevertheless, this tea steeper is an interesting and useful piece of silverwork which was copied from an antique piece.

The bowl is formed in the same manner as the oval saltcellar in Plate 28. The maple die shown at A, Plate 38, is similar to the one used for shaping the saltcellar, except that it needs to be somewhat larger for making this spoon.

After the bowls have been hammered out of 24-ga. silver, to the shape shown at B, cut off the edges and file the two halves to fit together. Form the hinge next by bending 24-ga. silver as shown at C, and solder it in place with medium solder. Saw off a small section D, and fit it into the large section as shown at E, Plate 38. For soldering, rest the bowl on the corner of a charcoal block, as shown at F, Plate 38, and lay the half hinge, bent to fit, in position. Then flux and add two snippets of solder. Allow the

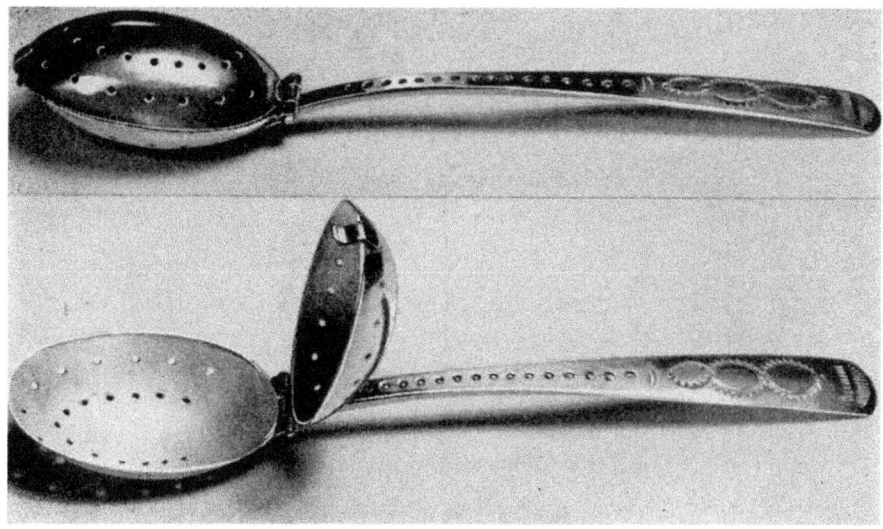

FIG. 55. Tea steeper

flux to dry before attempting to solder. When it has been soldered, paint the entire soldered portion with rouge, even forcing rouge into the hinge hole. Then rouge a piece of iron wire about the size of the pin. The reason for rouging also is to prevent solder from running where it is not wanted. Let the rouge dry first so that it will not mix with the flux. When the rouge has dried, put the other half of the hinge in place and insert the rouged iron pin. Then place the top half of the spoon in position, fit the hinge to it, and solder.

Next take out the iron hinge pin and solder the clasp on the upper half of the bowl. If no spring silver is on hand, use nickel silver for the clasp.

Make the handle out of a $\frac{1}{4}$-in. strip of 14-ga. silver. Hammer it flat for the upper end and on the edge for the narrow section. File out all irregularities, stamp it, and bend it to shape. Slightly dome the flattened section to give it more rigidity. Use rather heavy iron wire to hold the handle in place for soldering, and rouge the hinge to prevent the solder from melting.

At *H*, Plate 38, is shown a simple and efficient way of wiring. Drill the holes in the spoon bowls with a $\frac{1}{32}$-in. drill after which buff and polish both parts. Take off the burrs around the holes with a larger drill. Hold the drill between the fingers and give it a turn or two. Then buff and polish the entire steeper. Cut a piece of wire for the hinge joint, about $\frac{1}{16}$ in. longer than the hinge, and tap the wire lightly on both sides to upset it enough to prevent it from slipping out.

Unique Brooches

INDIAN silversmiths make many brooches nowadays, some of which are very unique. Some are naturalistic in design while others are more or less symbolic. The five shown in Plate 39 represent a fairly good cross section of the type of brooches made. While the butterflies in Plate 39 are symbolic, the lower June bug and the dragonfly are quite naturalistic, and the bird represents an abstract design. In fact, the bird looks as though it were made from a discarded silver button.

The bodies of the butterflies and the dragonfly are made of half-round

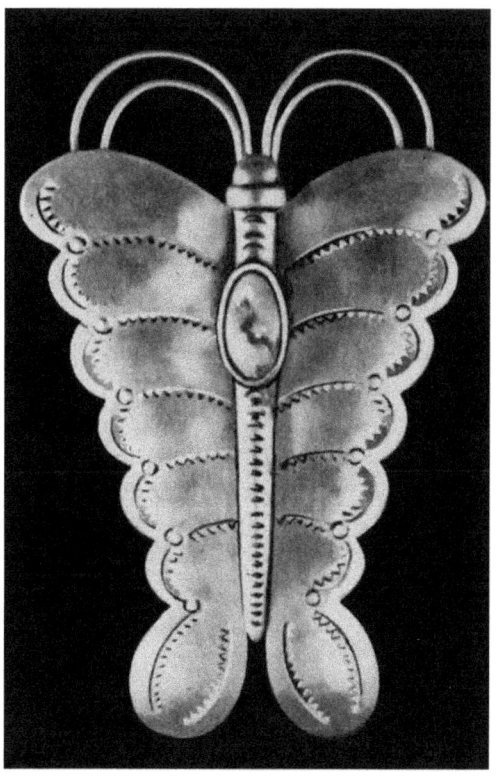

FIG. 56. Butterfly brooch

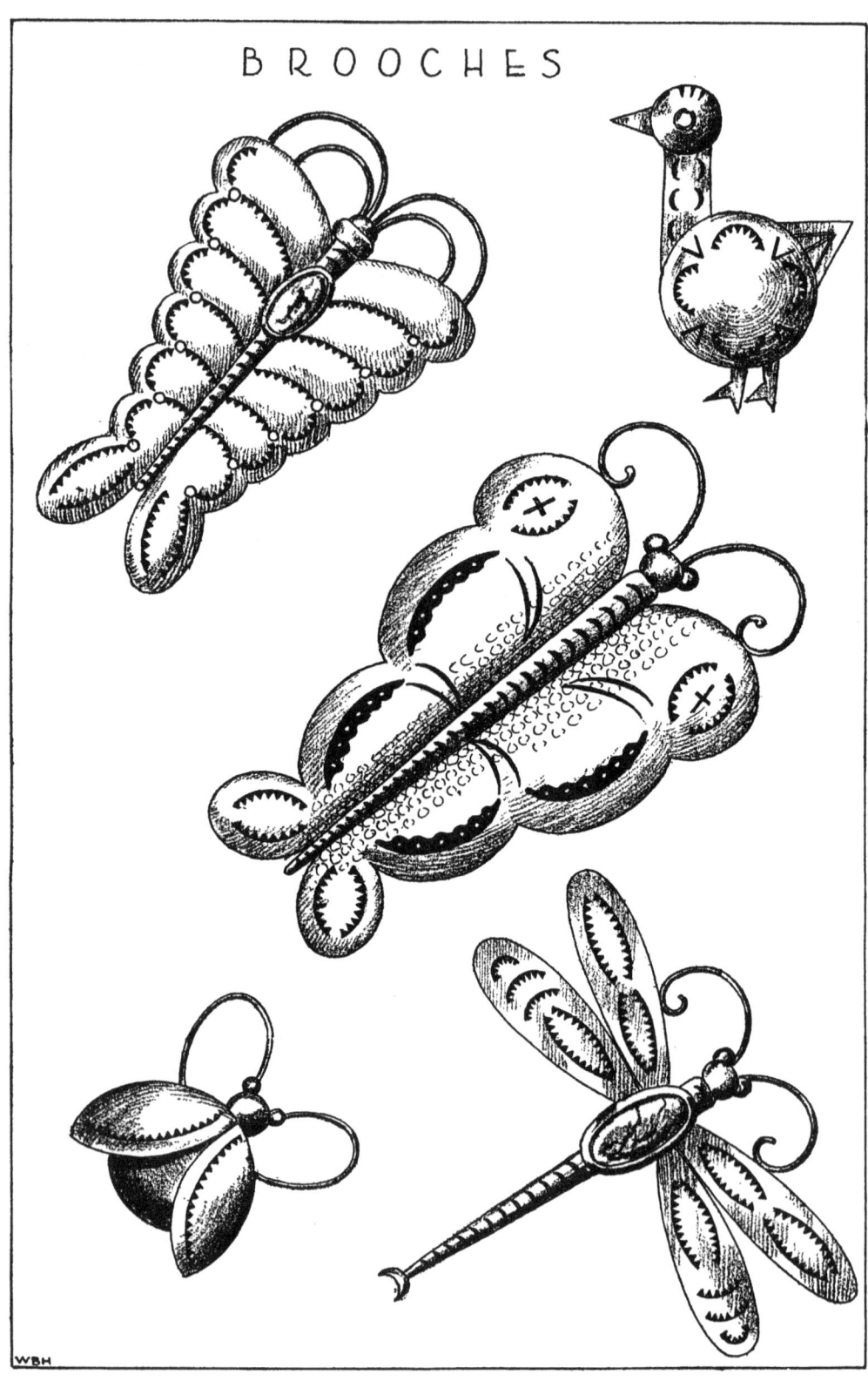

PLATE 39

wire, hammered and filed to the taper shown. A U-shaped piece of silver forms the eyes of the upper brooch, and the lower ones have the heads filed and the eyes soldered on later.

In the upper butterfly, the body is filed down to form a flat base for the setting. After the wings and the bodies of the butterflies have been stamped, they are soldered while still flat. The feelers are soldered below the head and wings. The slight rounding of the wings is done on a block of maple wood from the reverse side. The metal is hammered out with a stamp of $\frac{1}{2}$-in. round steel slightly rounded at the end. A stamp of maple wood also could be used. Do not use a ball-peen hammer. This would produce small bumps which cannot be filed out.

The wings of the dragonfly are left flat. The June bug is made with a dapped out half sphere for a body, and the head also is a small half sphere with raindrops soldered on for eyes. The wings are slightly less than one quarter spheres. They are set away from the body.

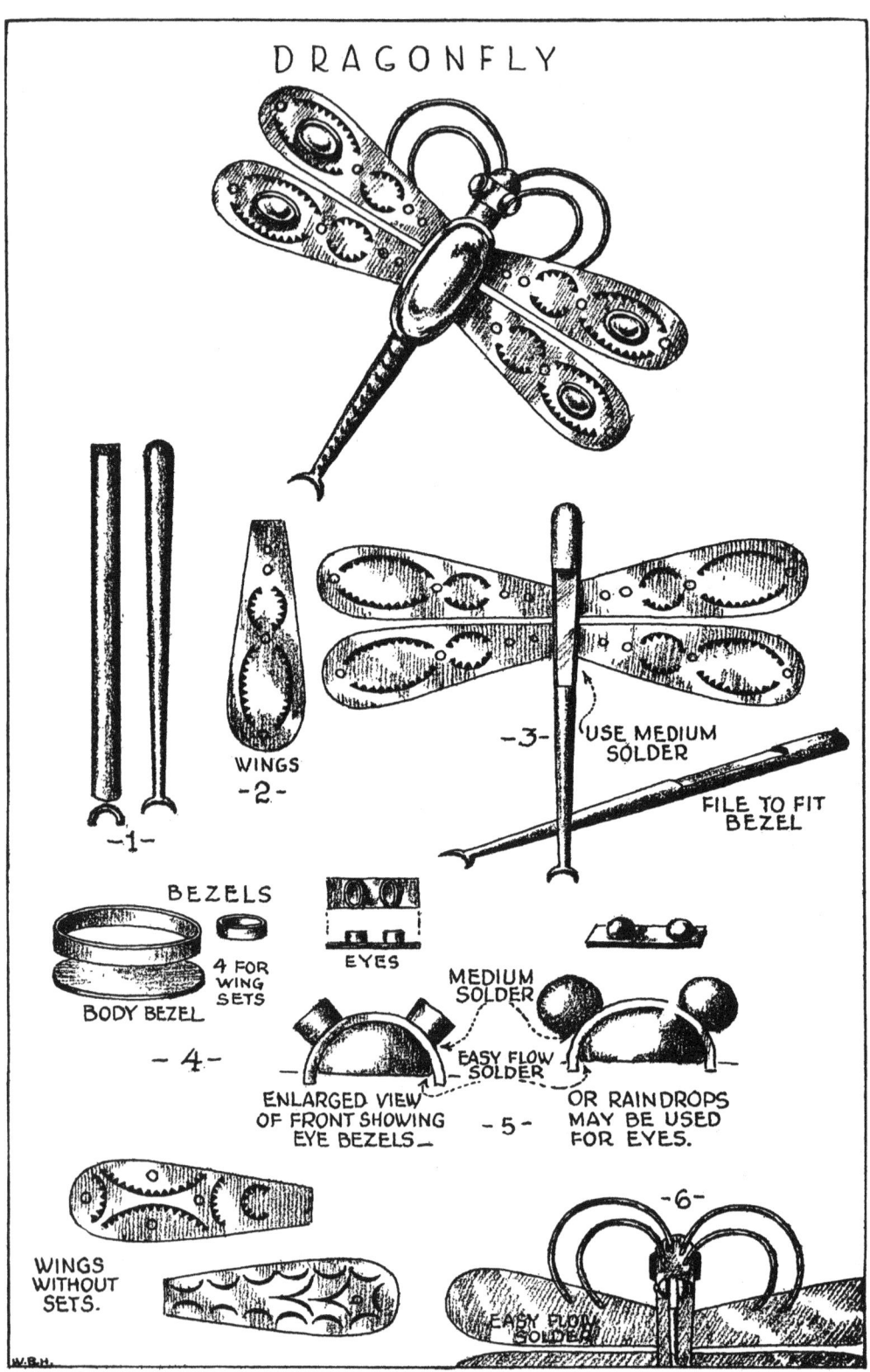

Dragonfly Brooch

THE dragonfly brooch in Plate 40 is rather elaborate and somewhat complicated, but when completed, it is a beautiful piece of jewelry. This brooch also can be made without the turquoise and still be attractive. The small stones and the large body stone were shaped on a carborundum wheel and finished with a sandpaper stick. They were then polished with tin oxide.

The parts were soldered together with easy-flowing and medium solder. Rouge must be applied to the soldered parts nearest the points where the last soldering is to be done.

To make this brooch, first hammer and file a piece of half-round wire for the body as shown in 1, Plate 40. Then solder the crescent-shaped end and file it to shape.

Cut out the wings and stamp them, as shown at 2. Determine the size of the large bezel and file a flat base for it on the body as shown at 3. Solder the wings to the body with medium-hard solder. Make such other

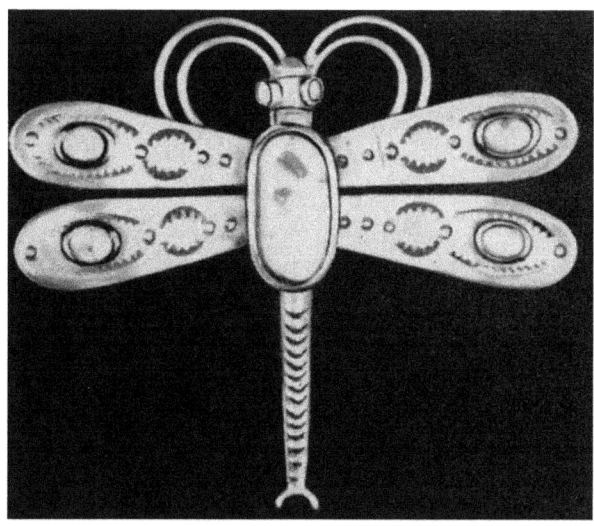

FIG. 57. Dragonfly brooch

bezels as are required. Make eyes. If small stones are on hand, solder small bezels to a strip of silver. If not, solder two raindrops on a strip for eyes with medium-hard solder as shown at 5, Plate 40. Bend the eyepiece strips to fit around the body. If necessary, file to get a good snug fit. Let the ends project until after soldering and then file them flush.

Solder the eyepiece and wing bezels in place with easy-flowing solder. The body bezel should be soldered together with medium-hard solder and then soldered to the body, in the same operation, with easy-flowing solder.

Shape the feelers. Lay the dragonfly bottom up, on a charcoal block. Scoop out a depression in the block for the body bezel, so that the parts will lie quite flat.

Solder the feelers and pin in one operation. Place a piece of charcoal or asbestos under the feelers to get them to lie level. Use easy-flowing solder, and rouge the soldered parts near the last soldering.

Set the stones. Give the entire pin a final polish.

Lapel Pins

PLATE 41 and Figure 58 show several lapel pins seen in Aztec, New Mexico. They are fine examples of modern Indian silversmithing.

Figure 58 shows a frog made by the author. Note the round eyes and the shaped stone for the body. The base includes the body and legs. To make this frog, saw out the base and stamp it. Stamp out the webbed feet with a blunt, rounded stamp, and finish with a small round or half-round file. Solder the large bezel onto the base. The sketch in the upper left-hand corner of Plate 41 shows how the head is fastened. Shape the head and solder the eye bezels in place. Then solder the little piece of angle silver to the head and to the under part of the body, leaving enough room for the body, which consists of a large turquoise. Bend the upright part of the angle piece out of the way when setting the large stone. Then bend it back into its former position. This must be done carefully, but it is not too difficult.

The wings of the large butterfly in Plate 41 are made in one piece. The body is made of sheet silver, stamped, and then bent over a piece of round metal and soldered. In bending the wing piece see that it fits the body. Then bump up the wings quite a bit. The head is a large solid raindrop and the eyes are small raindrops.

The grasshopper is made of 14 pieces. This is quite a job of soldering, but it makes a beautiful pin. The sketches in Plate 41 show how the bottom looks and how the legs are bent and attached. Turquoise stones are used for the eyes.

The bumblebee was made quite simply. The wings and bottom of the body are all in one with the domed-up body soldered to the base. The stamping is done before the forming.

The middle-sized butterfly to the right of the large one in Figure 58 is simplified still more. The body and wings are of one piece. The body is bumped up, the forward wings are bent up slightly, and the back wings are bent down. This butterfly is made of 24-ga. silver. A raindrop

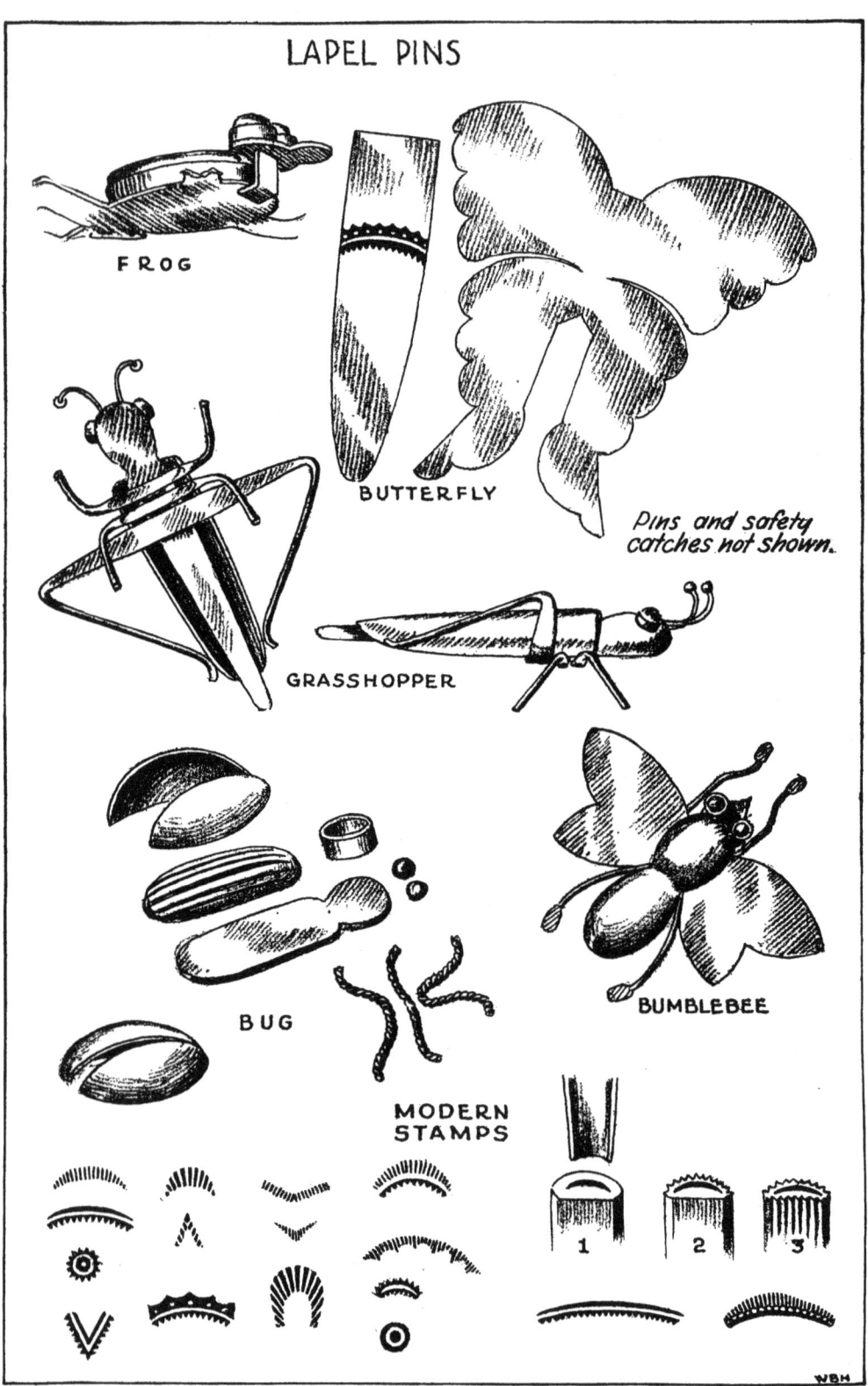

is soldered between the wings to hold them more rigid. The eyes are small turquoise and the nose is a raindrop.

The large bug to the right of the frog in Figure 58 is a little more complicated, as shown by the sketches in Plate 41. These bugs may be made without turquoise, a domed piece of silver taking the place of the stone. The wings are made by cutting a domed circular piece almost in two down the middle.

The rest of the pieces in Figure 58 are rather easily made. The owl's wings are sweated onto the body, and the beak and ear pieces are sweated onto the head.

All of the designs are made with modern stamps shown in Plate 41.

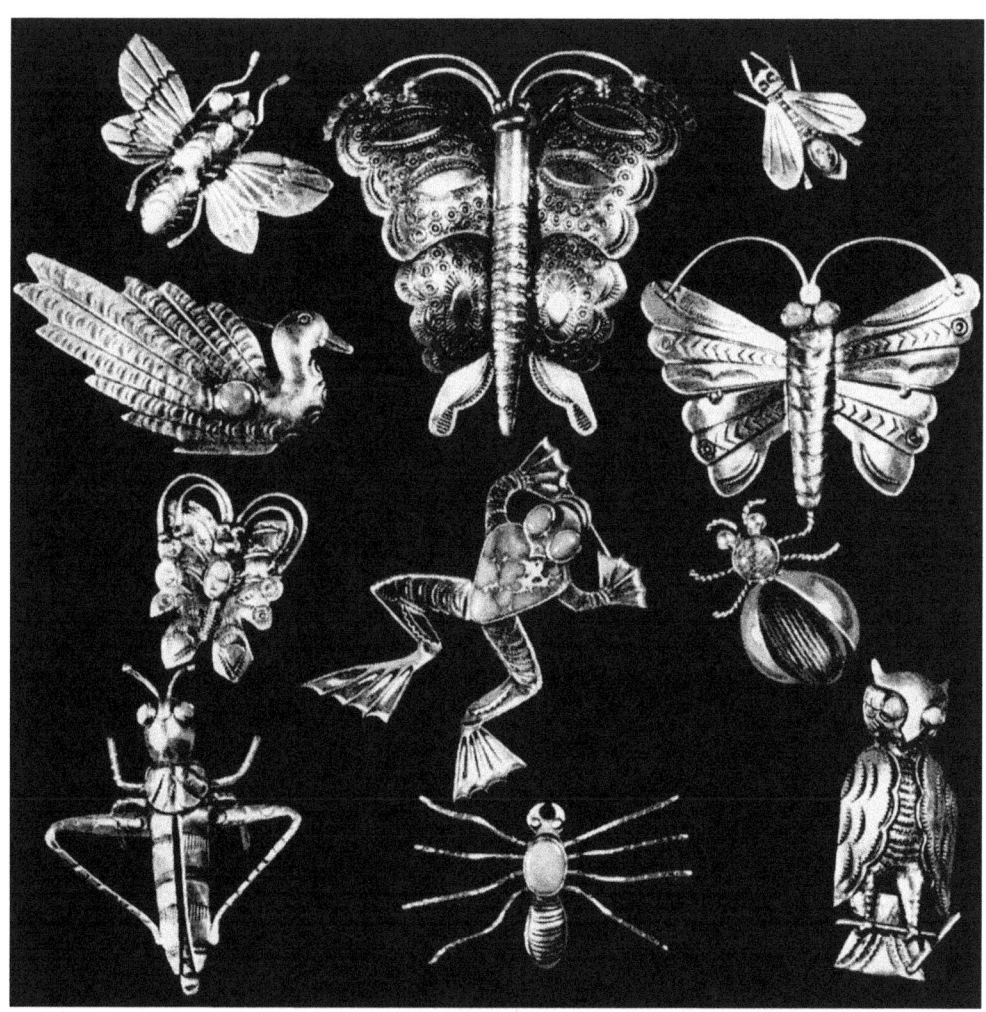

FIG. 58. Indian pieces photographed through the courtesy of Dean Kirk, Aztec Ruins Trading Post, Aztec, N. Mex.

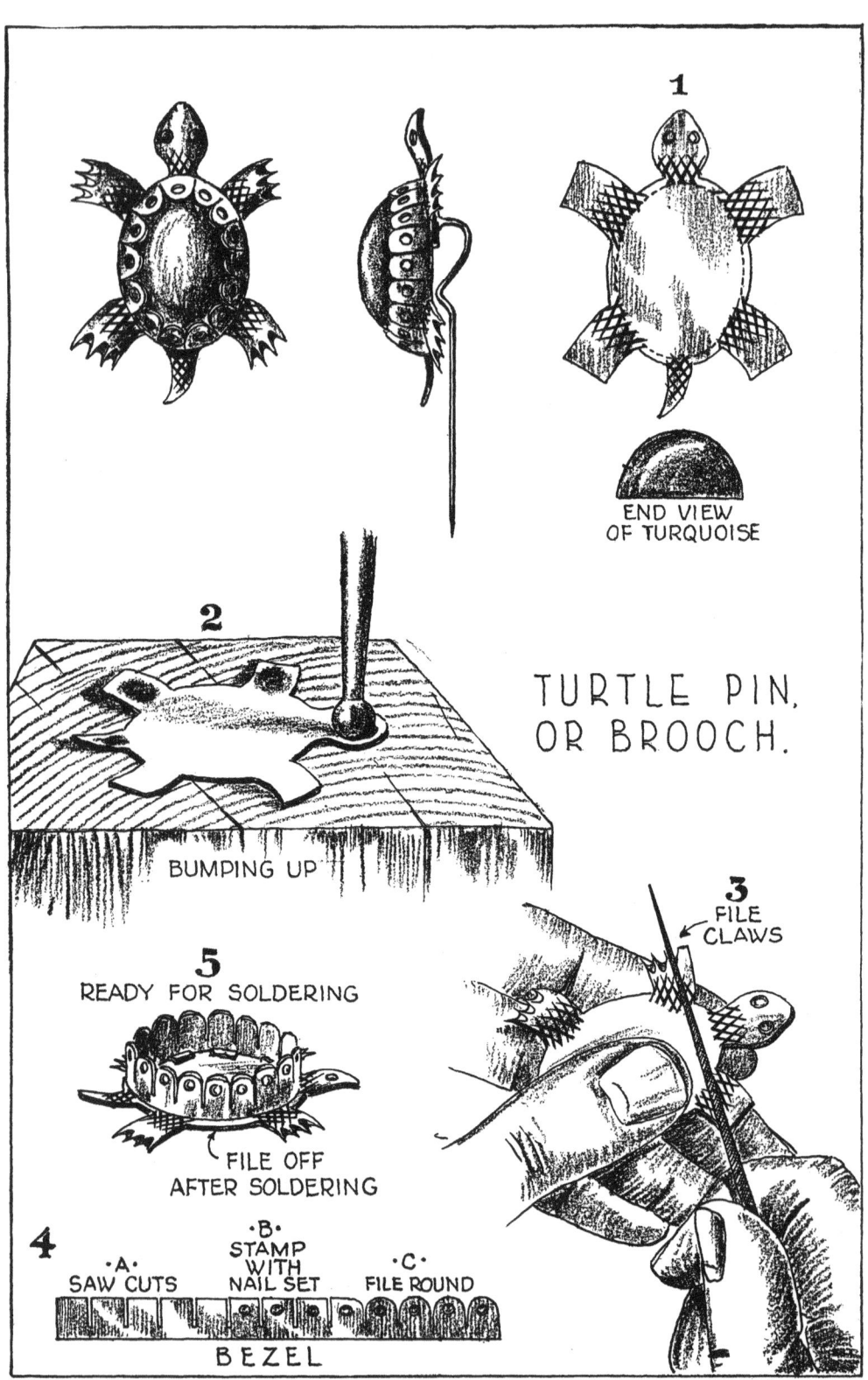

PLATE 42

Turquoise Turtle Pin

THE shape of a given piece of turquoise often determines or suggests the setting or the use to which it may be put. In this instance the high cabochonlike stone had the general shape of a box turtle shell; hence, it was used to make a turtle pin.

This stone, incidentally, was ground on a 4-in. hand-power grinding wheel and polished with tin oxide on a piece of buckskin, as described on pages 51 to 55, and Figures 15 to 20.

To carry out the shell effect on the turtle in a symbolic way, the bezel was made much higher than is customary and filed and stamped as shown.

To make this pin, cut the blank, allowing about $\frac{1}{16}$ in. to project beyond the bezel where no legs, head, or tail are. This will later be filed flush with the base of the bezel. Do the crosshatch stamping with a fine lining tool. Punch the eyes with a fine nail set, or solder on raindrops instead. After stamping the blank, turn it over on a block of wood, and, with a small dapping punch, bump up the head and legs slightly. Don't file the claws too sharp, and bend them down somewhat to prevent them from catching on the clothing.

Saw out the bezel shown at 4 and 5, Plate 42, then stamp it, and file it round. Do not use too fine a saw blade or the scallops will not fit over the stone as they should. After the bezel has been completed, solder it to the base and file the base even with the bezel. A pin with a safety catch may be used instead of the one shown in Plate 42, although this sort of pin is much easier to make and fasten to the lapel.

FIG. 59. Silver turtle pin or brooch

Squash-Blossom Necklaces

ONE of the most attractive pieces of jewelry made by the Indians is the squash-blossom necklace. It is controversial whether the so-called blossom has been taken from the sunflower, the pomegranate, or the squash, but we shall call it by its old name — the squash blossom.

There are three separate parts to these necklaces — the beads, the squash blossoms, and the pendant. The Navahos usually make their necklaces rather plain with perhaps a turquoise or two set in the pendant, while the Zuni use more turquoise decoration and make their squash blossoms much more elaborately. The necklaces shown in Figures 60 and 61 are fine examples of Zuni work. Since good turquoise always is rather expensive, this article dwells mostly on the plainer types of necklaces.

Hollow Silver Beads

The first step in making a necklace is to learn how to make hollow beads. Making hollow beads by the method described here is relatively simple. A close study of the beads in the accompanying illustrations will show that they are not round. This distinguishes them from factory-made beads which are perfectly round. Indian silversmiths made beads by stamping them out with wooden dies which is the reason why they were flat. Therefore, when making beads for an Indian necklace do not become discouraged if they are not perfectly round.

The steps in making beads are shown in Plate 43. Use thin silver, say 24 ga. Cut a disk as shown at 1, Plate 43, a little larger than the size required. Beads usually are from $3/16$ to $5/16$ in. in diameter. Make one bead to determine how large to cut the disk. After stamping it out on a wood block or on a dapping die, as shown at 2, file the edges even as shown at 3, and punch a hole in the center of each half. Punch the center hole as shown at 4, and file off the rough ends after punching as shown at 5. Do not file the protruding metal down to the bead proper, however, but leave a little of it stand, as shown at 9. Ream out the hole to prevent its cutting the cord. When a number of half beads have been

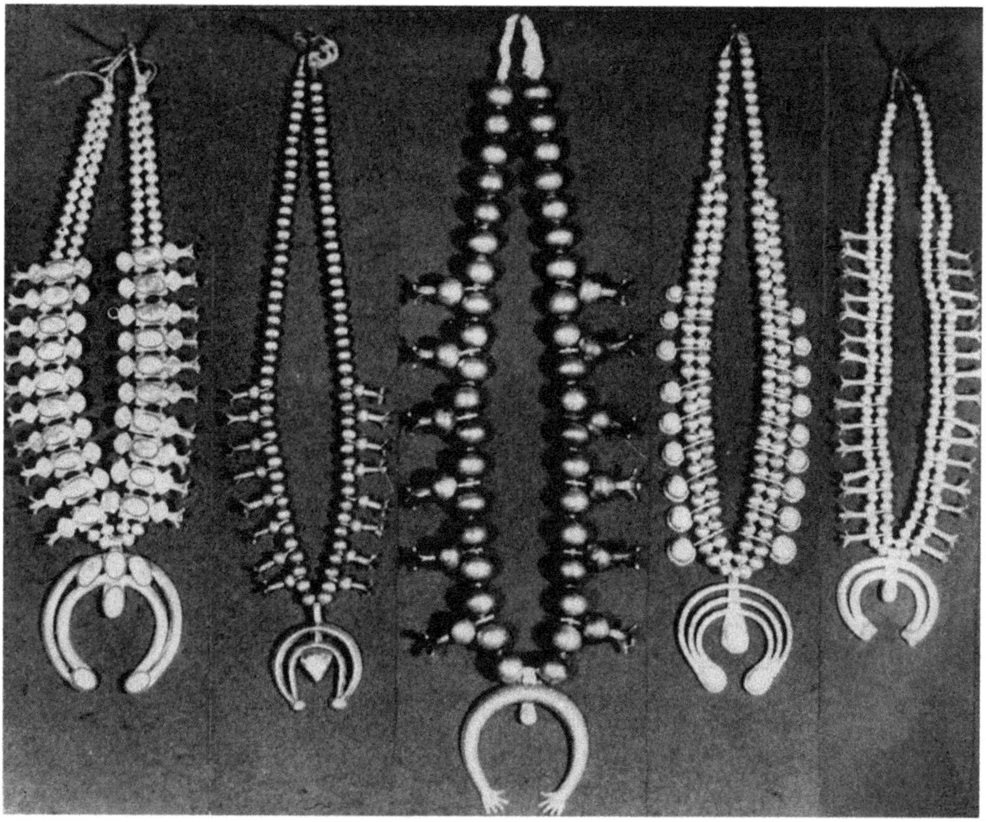

FIG. 60. A variety of squash-blossom necklaces from the collection of Buck Burshears. The one on the left is Zuni

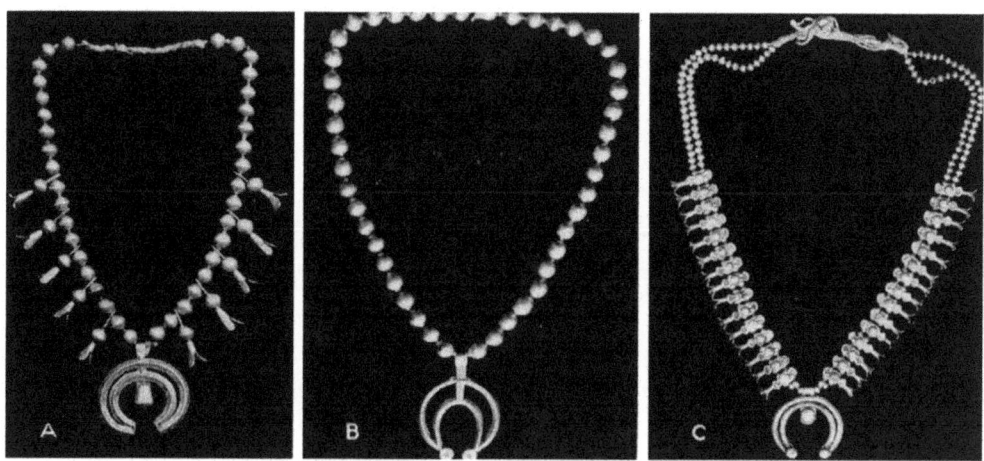

FIG. 61. A and B. Navaho necklaces. C. Zuni necklace
(Courtesy The Taylor Museum, Colorado Springs, Colo.)

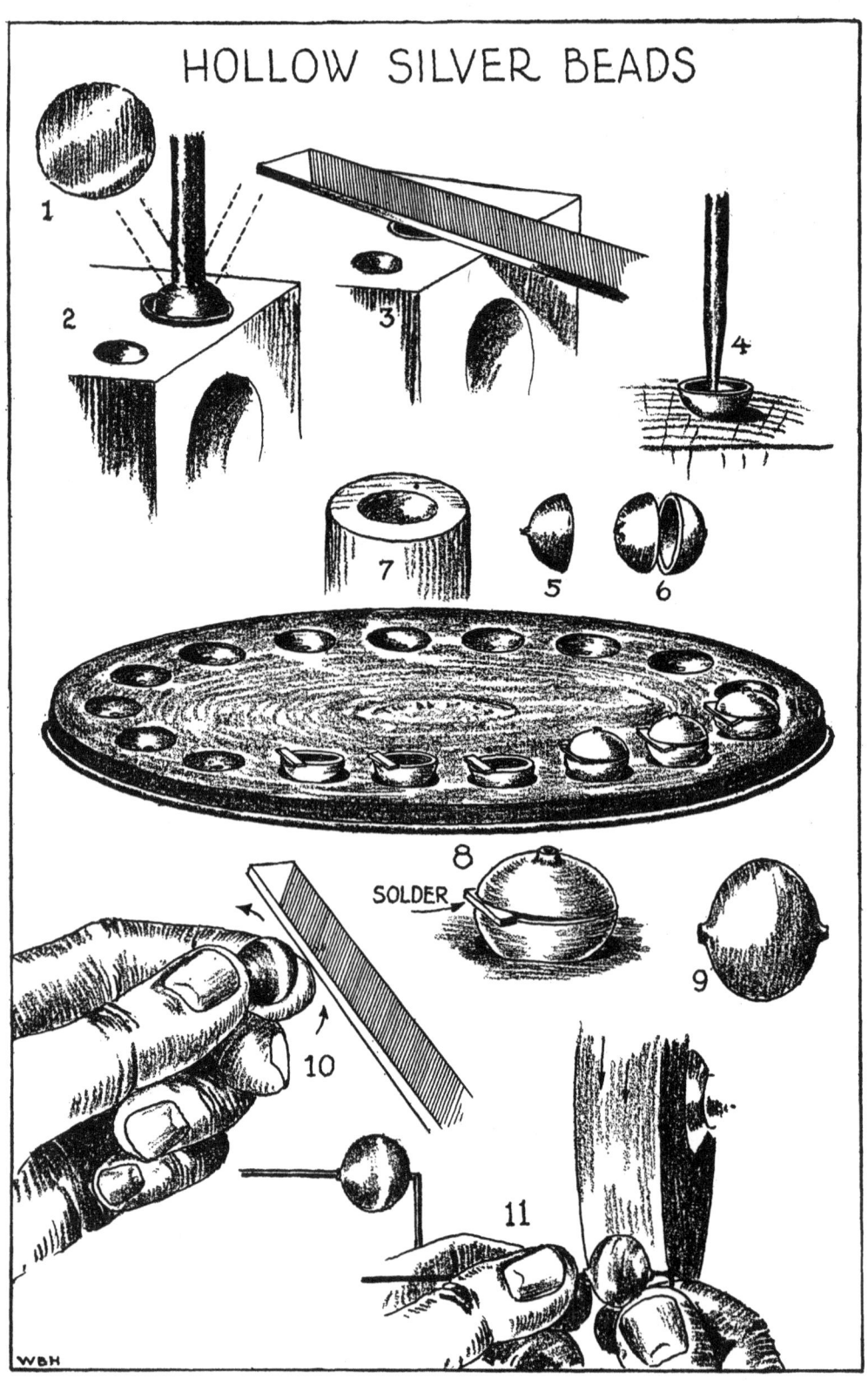

PLATE 43

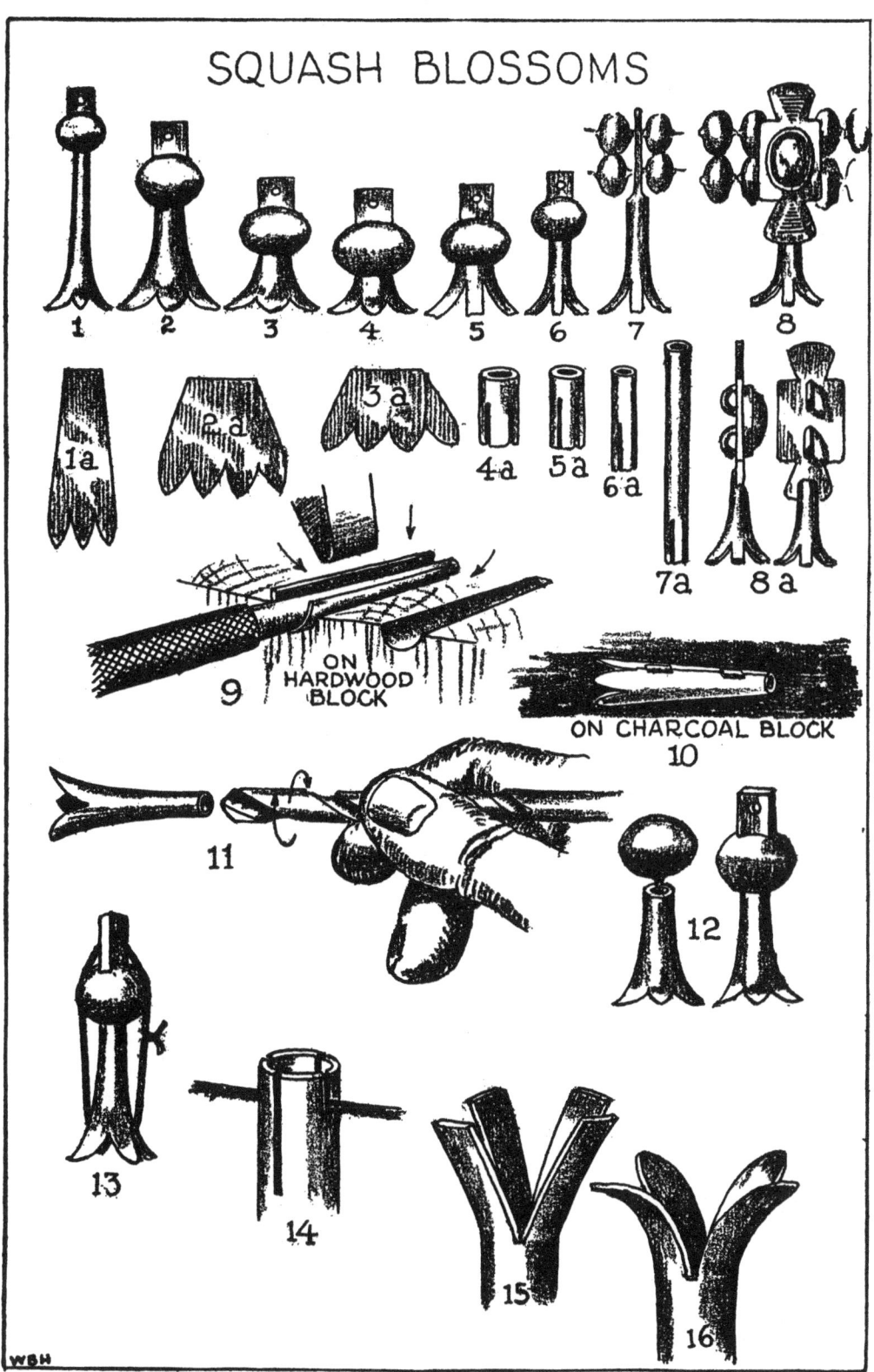

PLATE 44

finished, match them up in pairs as the different halves will vary slightly in diameter.

To facilitate the soldering, take a cover from a half-gallon can, such as a syrup can, and punch depressions in it as shown at 8 in Plate 43.

To form these depressions, cut and shape a hardwood block as shown at 7, and use that as a die. The depressions should be about $3/8$ in. in diameter and they need not be too deep. Punch a $1/16$-in. hole in the center of each depression to take the protrusion of the hole in the bead.

Place the half beads in the depressions, and flux the edges. Then lay a piece of solder across one edge, put flux on the top half, and set it in place over the bottom half. Even up the edges. When all have been set, apply the heat slowly. It is well to have all of the solder snippets on the left side of the beads; then apply most of the heat to the right. The solder will follow the heat, and after the first bead is soldered, the next one is just about hot enough so that one bead can be soldered after another. This all sounds easy, and it is, if the metal is clean and properly fluxed. Drop all of the beads in the pickle. Remove them and rinse them thoroughly in clean water to which ammonia has been added to neutralize any sulphuric acid that might be inside the beads. When the hot beads are thrown into the pickle, they fill up with acid, and if any of it is left inside, it will later on make the bead look as though it had a green eye. So rinse the beads carefully and thoroughly, and dry them well. File the solder joint as shown at 10, Plate 43, and then buff the beads as shown at 11. Buff each bead separately. A tip of a finger or thumb pressed against the bead prevents it from spinning on the wire.

Squash Blossoms

The regular and most common squash blossom is composed of three parts — the bead, the trumpet, and the eye, as shown in Plate 44. The Zuni type of blossom also is shown on Plates 7 and 8. The beads, as a rule, are the same size as the necklace beads except that a hole is punched through only one of the halves. The blossoms shown at 1, 2, and 3, Plate 44, are made with a tapered trumpet. A template cut out of cardboard or tin is used to cut out the blanks. The trumpets 4 to 8 are made of tubing which is hammered around a piece of metal, and then soldered along the seam. The petals are made by sawing as shown at 14, Plate 44. The blossoms at 1, 2, and 3 are formed with the aid of a suitable nail set and a groove cut into the end of a block of hardwood, as shown at 9, Plate 44. After the ends have been evenly butted, solder each trumpet as shown at 10, Plate 44. Then file the small end evenly, and ream the hole with a small twist drill as shown at 11. Bend the petals outward, and file them to shape. The eyes are merely small square or oblong pieces of heavier silver with a hole drilled for the cord.

All of these parts must fit perfectly for soldering whether they are to be wired together or not. The parts of the squash blossoms of the first necklace made by the author were soldered without wiring, by setting the trumpet part on a charcoal or asbestos block and setting in the bead, as shown at 12, Plate 44. The small protruding ends caused by punching the hole tend to seat the bead rather firmly. A slight twisting action with a little pressure usually causes the bead to set *tightly* in the trumpet. A small snippet of solder is set between the two parts, and the flux, when dry, helps to hold the parts in place.

The loops or eyes also must be fluxed and then set in place for soldering.

If the same solder is used for soldering the beads and assembling the parts, the soldered joints on the beads should be protected against the heat by painting them with rouge. The most satisfactory method of soldering is to use a medium solder followed with easy solder.

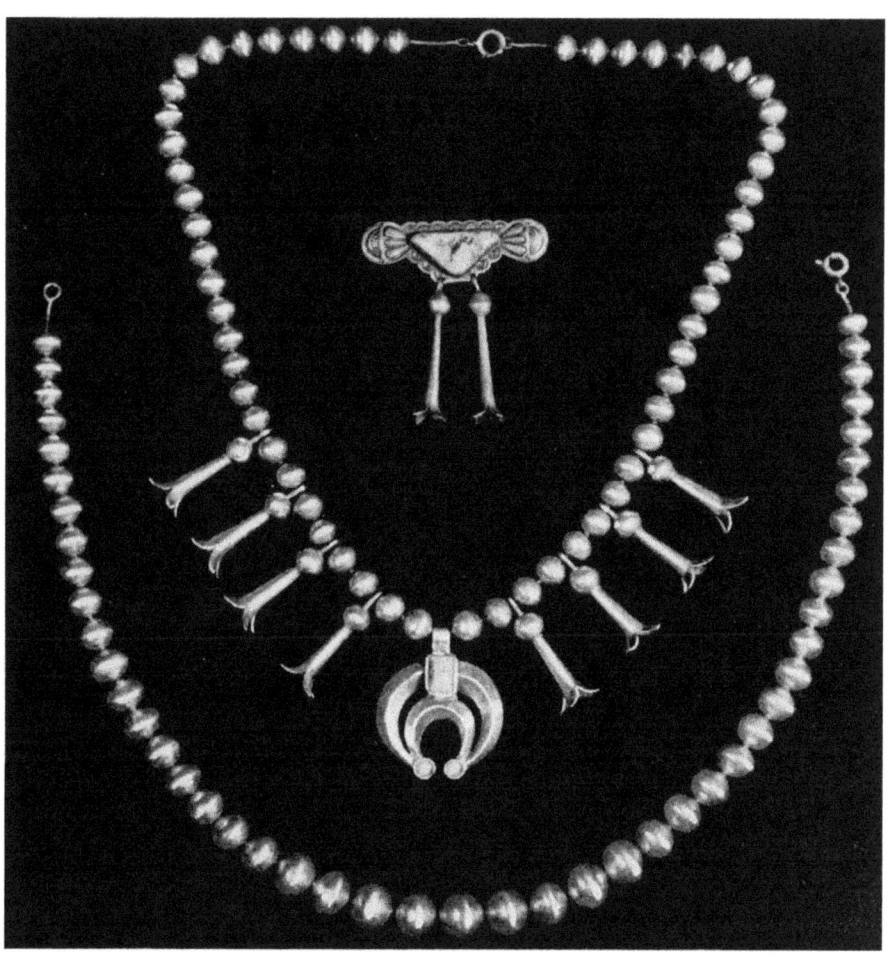

FIG. 62. Necklaces and brooch made by the author

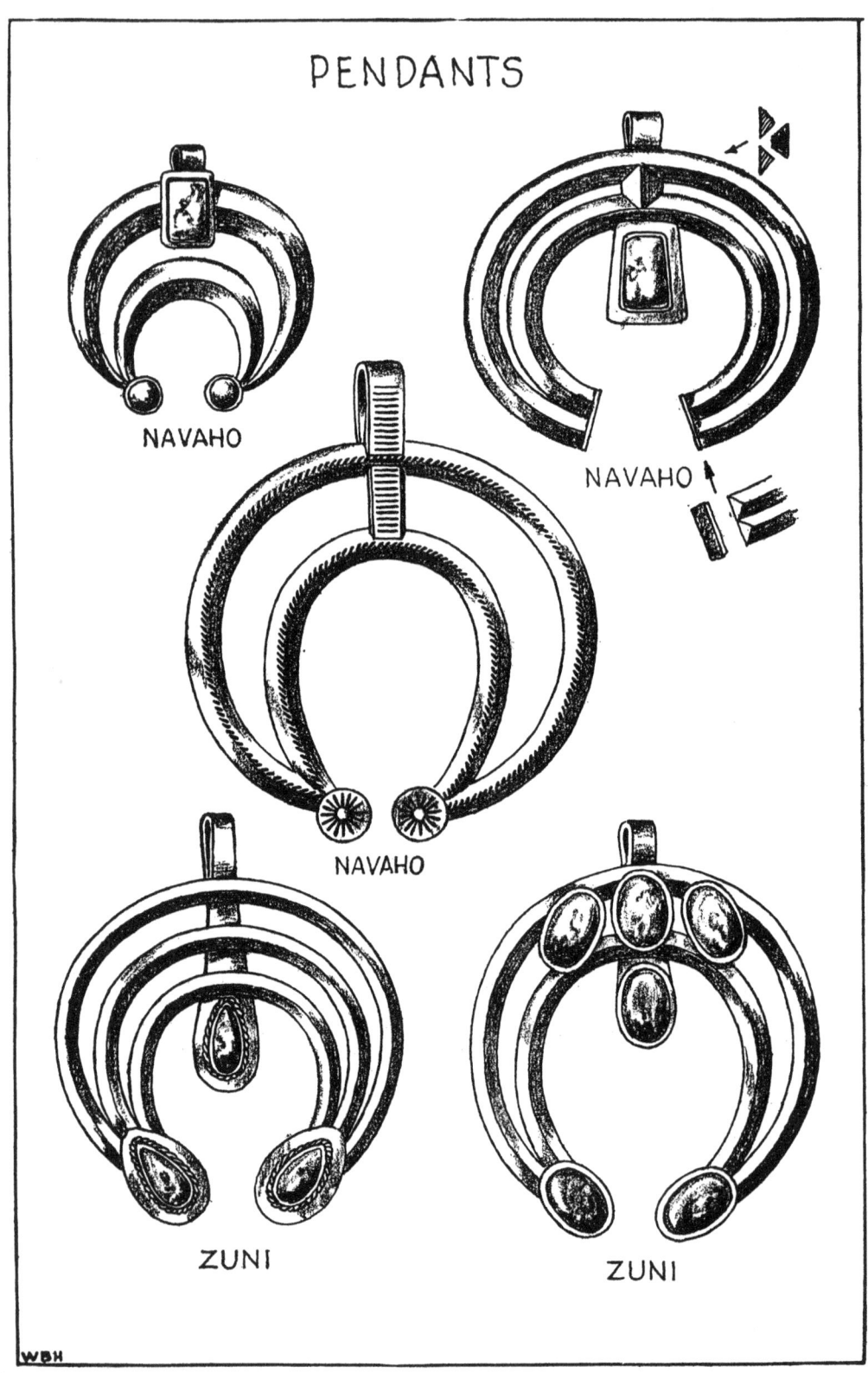

PLATE 45

At 13, Plate 44, a wired assembly is shown. Some prefer this method of holding the parts for soldering, but wiring requires great patience. When wiring, be careful not to twist the iron wire too tight. Have it just tight enough to hold the three pieces together. A slight kink in the wire on one or both sides will tighten it still more.

The Zuni squash blossom, shown at 8, Plate 44, is quite frequently used and is simple to make. The trumpet is of the tubular type, flattened at the top to fit the upper part. Any shape of turquoise may be used. At 7, Plate 44, is shown a tubular trumpet flattened at the upper end through which holes are drilled for the cord. This squash blossom really is only the trumpet part but tends to make an interesting necklace as shown at C, Figure 61. The first project in silversmithing attempted by the author was the squash-blossom necklace shown in Figure 62. The soldering was done with a blowtorch.

Pendants

Of the five pendants in Plate 45, the first one was cast in a dentist's gray investment, which is a heat-resisting material. The other four were made of triangular wire which is an easier and quicker method. A pendant similar to the one that was cast can be made by filing triangular wire. About the only thing that might be added in the way of explanation is that when mounting stones over the wire, file down where the mount rests on the wire, or hammer down the seat of the mount with a flat-nosed punch.

Stringing Beads

These necklaces are best strung on foxtail chain which can be bought at jewelers' supply houses. Good linen thread can be used, but be sure there are no sharp edges in the holes to fray the thread. Indians frequently place a knot in the string between each of the beads, so that if the thread or cord breaks, only one bead can be lost.

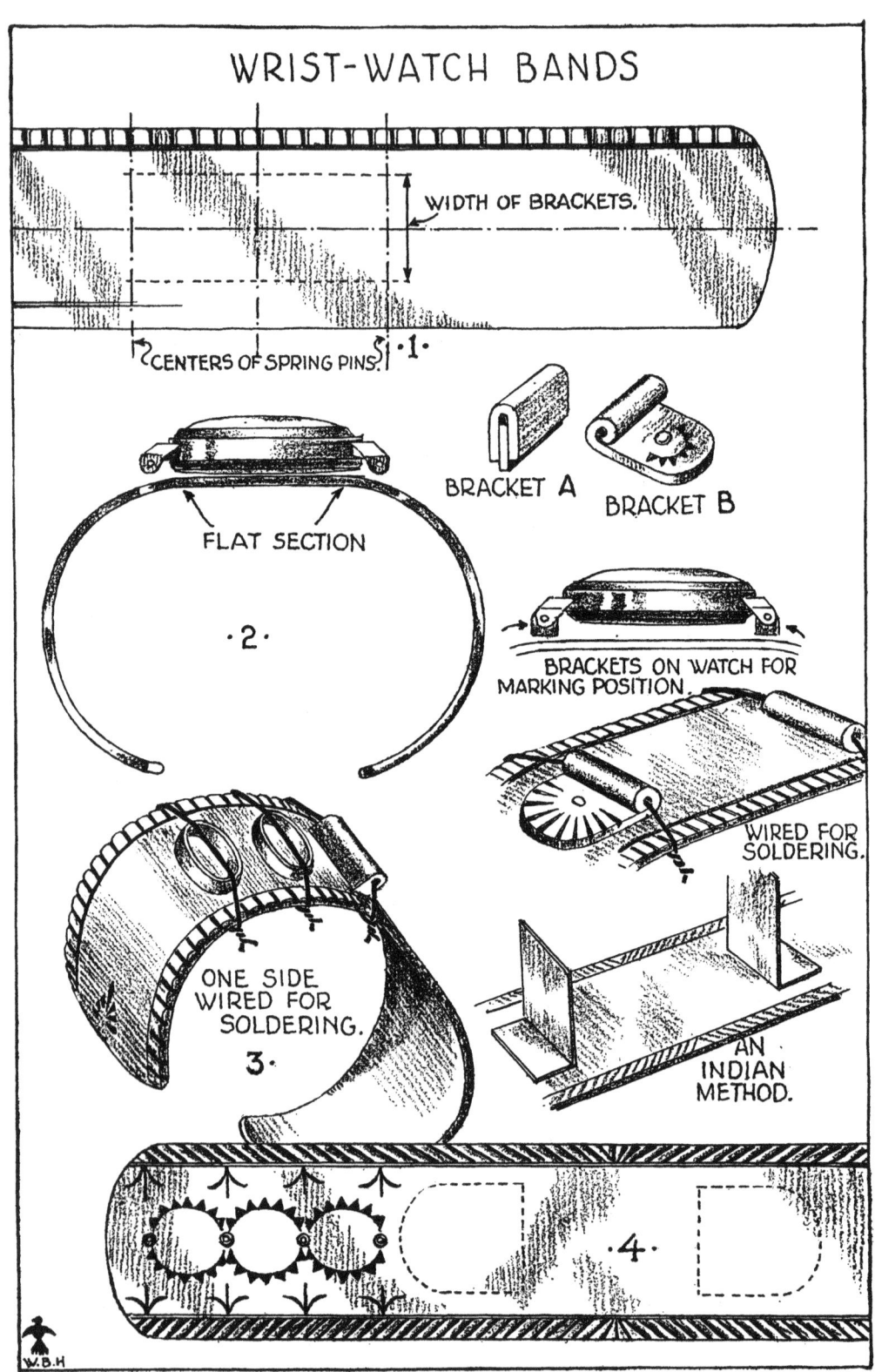

PLATE 46

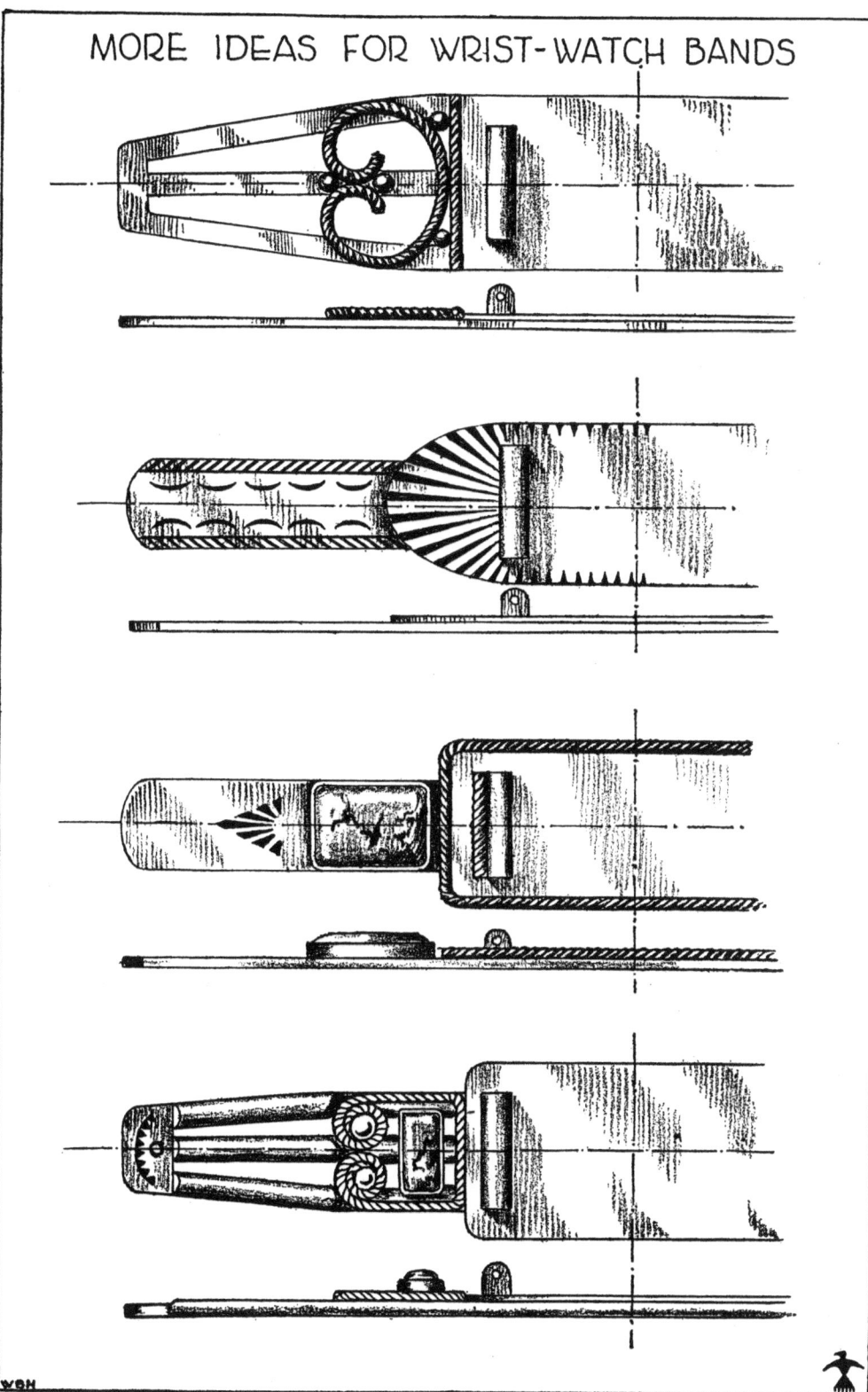

PLATE 47

Wrist-Watch Bands

THE idea of wearing a clamp-on watch band may not appeal to many people. After one has been worn, however, the individual may never want to replace it with another type of band.

When making one of these watch bands, be sure the band fits the wrist comfortably before soldering the brackets which hold the watch in place. Merely soldering brackets to a bracelet will not do. The bracelet must fit snugly. If the bracket grip is too light, or if the silver in the band is not heavy enough, the bracelet will break in time because of the slight bending of the metal when putting it on or removing it day after day.

Use 14-ga. silver, and make the width of the band so the winding stem projects for easy winding and setting. If a 6-in. blank makes a band that is too long, cut off some at the ends.

When an Indian makes a watch band he solders two pieces of silver to

FIG. 63.   Silver and spiderweb
turquoise watch band

the band, which project as shown in the lower right-hand portion of Plate 46. These two pieces of thin silver then are bent and fitted to the watch. At *A* and *B*, Plate 46, are shown two types of brackets that are soldered in the correct position.

Bracket *A* is made of 14-ga. silver. It consists of a U-shaped piece with another piece of 14-ga. silver soldered inside. Ream or drill out the opening to fit the spring pin in the watch. The sketch showing bracket *B* is self-explanatory. This bracket also should be made of 14-ga. silver. Bend it around a nail the size of the spring pin of the watch, and later ream it to fit. When the brackets have been made, attach them to the watch and find their exact position on the band. Then stamp the band. This procedure is not necessary on the upper band, Plate 46, because the ornament does not conflict with the brackets or the settings. After stamping, buff and polish the band, and then bend it to fit the wrist. Next, place a *thin* piece of cardboard on the band under the watch, and file the brackets so that they fit properly. Curve the long brackets to fit the band. The watch should fit without making it necessary to bend the band to insert the pins. Mark the exact position of each bracket with a fine scriber. Remove the brackets from the watch, and wire them in place for soldering. Brackets *A* and *B* can be soldered at the same time, but in the case of the other band, proceed as shown in 3. Wire the bezels and the bracket on one side, and solder them in the position shown. Then clean up the other side and do likewise. Prop up the bracelet with pieces of charcoal when soldering.

Many types of bracelets can be used for wrist-watch bands. The two bands shown in Figures 63 and 64 were chosen mainly to show the

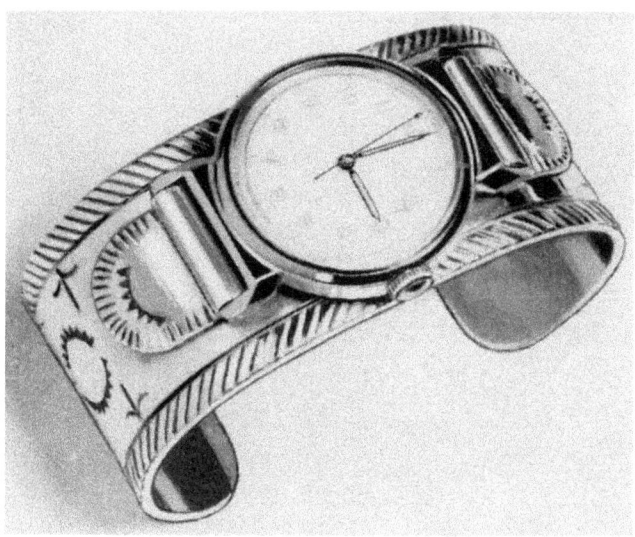

FIG. 64. Aluminum watch band

method of construction rather than for beauty of design. Bear in mind not to have the watch setting too high. Keep it as low as possible, and do not make the band of silver too light or the constant bending may eventually cause it to crystallize and break. Remember, also, to be consistent, do not place a gold watch on a silver band.

Plate 47 shows a few more good wrist-watch band designs.

Miniature Vases and Canteens

THE miniature vases and canteens in Plate 48 and Figures 65 and 66 are simple to make. They represent some of the popular modern pieces made by the Indians. The boutonnière vases are, as may be seen in the drawings, only half vases, and therefore, not as difficult to make as though they were in the round. Make the half-round sphere first. Then make the neck from an oblong piece of silver hammered to shape in a form cut out of a piece of hardwood as shown at 3, Plate 48. The finished shape of the neck is shown at 2. Cut or file an opening in the half sphere, and file the bowl and the neck to a snug fit. Cut out the back larger than the finished piece,

FIG. 65. Boutonnière

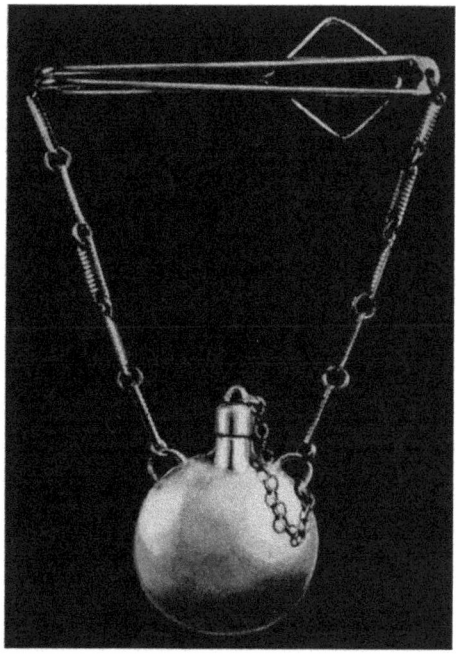

FIG. 66. Canteen tie clasp

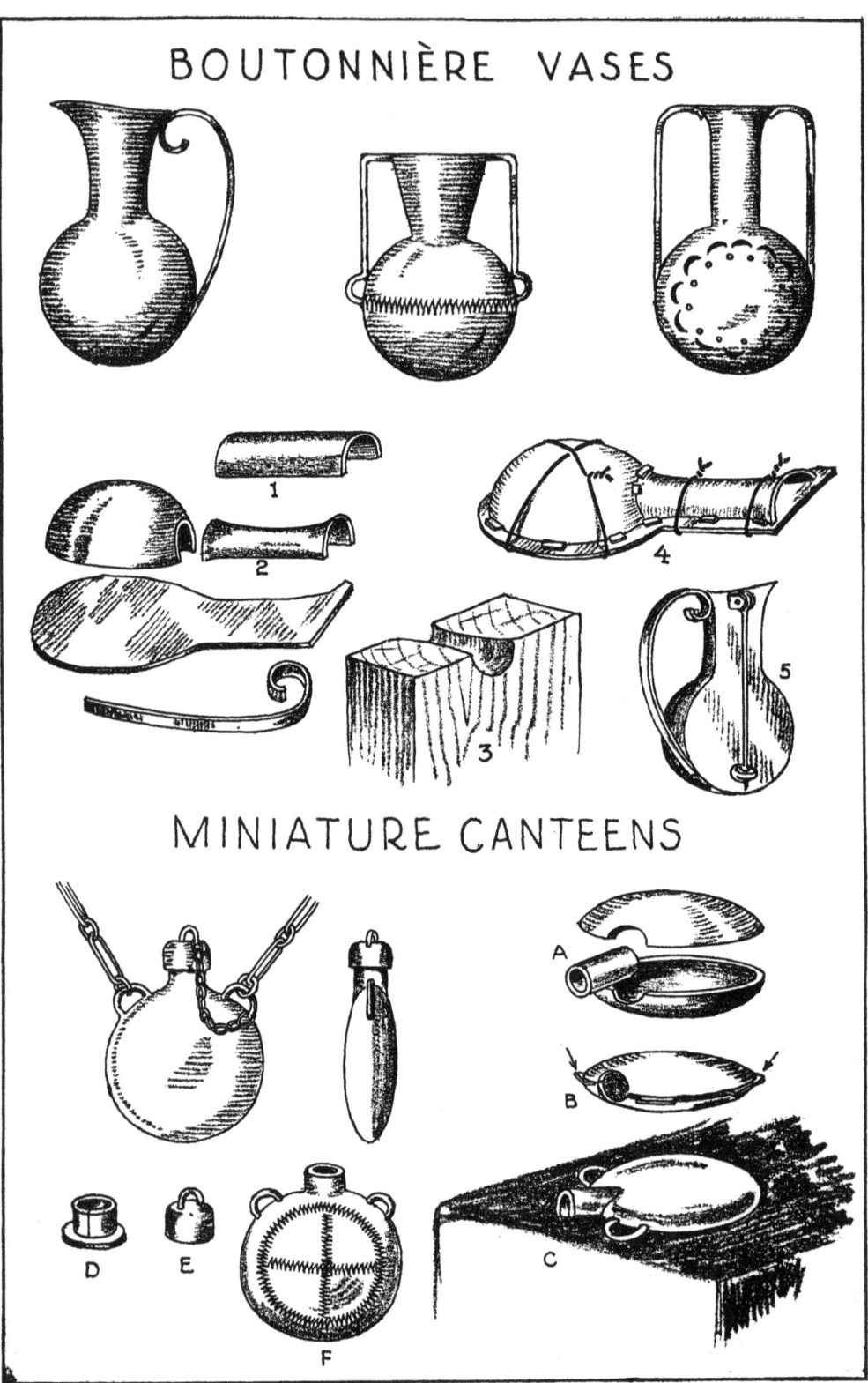

PLATE 48

and wire for soldering as shown at 4. After soldering, cut and file the edges and buff the vase. Then add the handle, and solder the pin to the back. The reason for buffing before the handle has been attached is that it is easier then to polish the section under the handle. The handle is made of a strip of 20-ga. silver but it also can be made of wire.

Sometimes these vases are ornamented with jiggle engraving which is done last, and occasionally stamped ornaments are used. These ornaments are stamped before forming as is done in making buttons.

The miniature canteens are used for pendants on necktie clasps. As shown, a plain chain clasp may be used, and the canteen is inserted in the middle of the chain. To make the canteen, solder together the two shallow halves, shown at A, Plate 47, with medium solder as when making hollow beads, and then solder the joint in the neck, the neck to the body, and the two loops for the chain, in one operation. To make the job easier, hollow out a block of charcoal, as shown at C, so that the neck and loops all lie in one plane. This prevents any chance of shifting. To make the cap, form the cylinder to size, and solder it. Then try it for a fit. If too large, make another cap, and if too small, ream it out to fit the neck. Set the ring on top in place and solder it as shown at D and E. Fasten a piece of delicate chain to the cap and one side loop so that the cap will not be lost. These canteens also may be decorated with jiggle engraving or with small round turquoise sets. Formerly, the Navaho made canteens about 5 in. in diameter for use as tobacco pouches.

Emery Polishing Stick

AFTER having used an emery stick on your jewelry or art metalwork, you will wonder how you ever got along without one. Emery paper can be used for a number of things. For jewelry work a fine polishing paper does the most satisfactory work, and while it does not polish, it is very satisfactory for the step before polishing. File marks and fine scratches can be easily removed with it. This emery stick is so made that when the paper is worn too smooth, that first layer can be torn off and three new layers are underneath ready for use.

The stick itself can be anywhere from ½ to ¾ in. square, or rectangular. The one shown is $9/16$ in. square, which seems to be a good size for Indian silversmithing.

Begin by laying the stick exactly along one edge of the abrasive paper

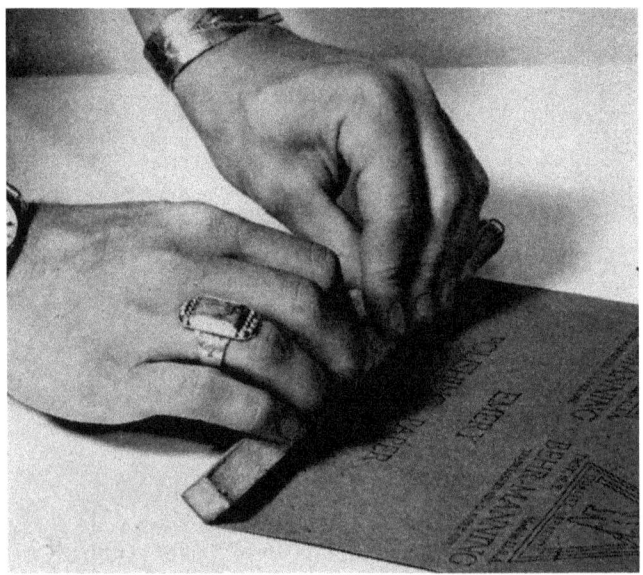

FIG. 67. Starting to fold the abrasive cloth or paper around the stick

as shown in Figure 67. Then hold the stick down firmly and score the emery paper with any smooth, slightly dulled tool, such as a dull kitchen knife, as shown in Figure 68. Fold over the edge of the paper by rolling the stick, and score for the next edge, as in Figure 69. Continue doing

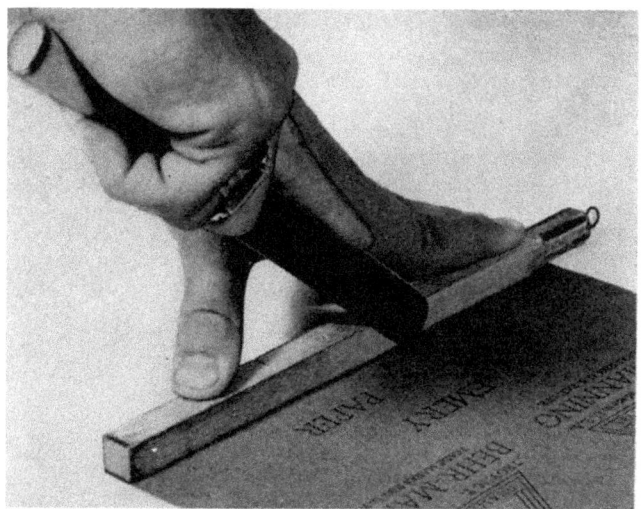

FIG. 68. Creasing the abrasive cloth or paper before making the first fold

this until the sheet of emery paper is rolled onto the stick. The emery paper usually is cut off after the last lap has overlapped the beginning. Thus, when you are down to the last of the paper, the two edges are fastened to the stick. One working face out of four is lost, but there is

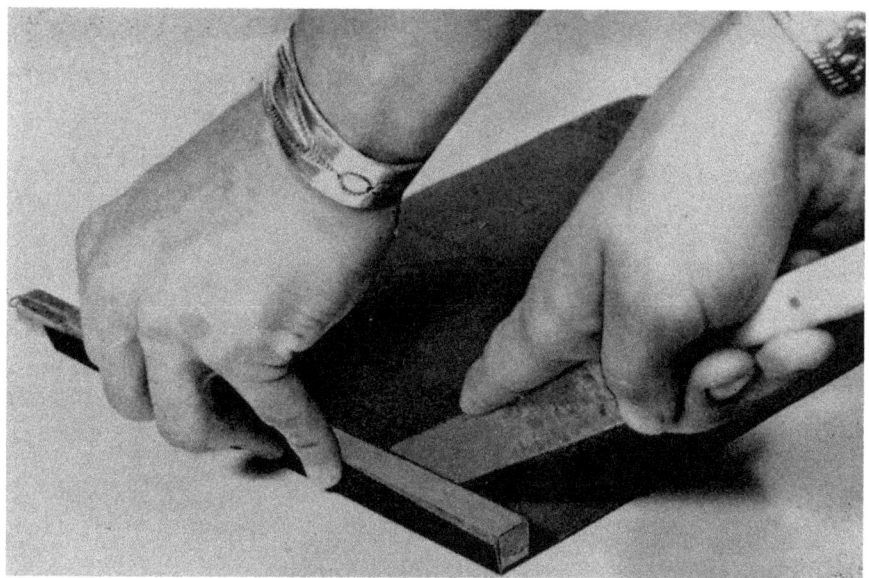

FIG. 69. Making a crease before the next fold

no other waste. Fastening the paper can be done with tacks, small nails, or by stapling, as shown in Figure 70. Small nails, cut off to about ½ in., can be countersunk slightly making the nailed side usable. But the nailheads must be below the surface of the emery paper.

Do not use a good silver knife for scoring the paper. The knife used is pressed against the gritty side of the paper which would wear down the blade after the first round of paper is on the stick.

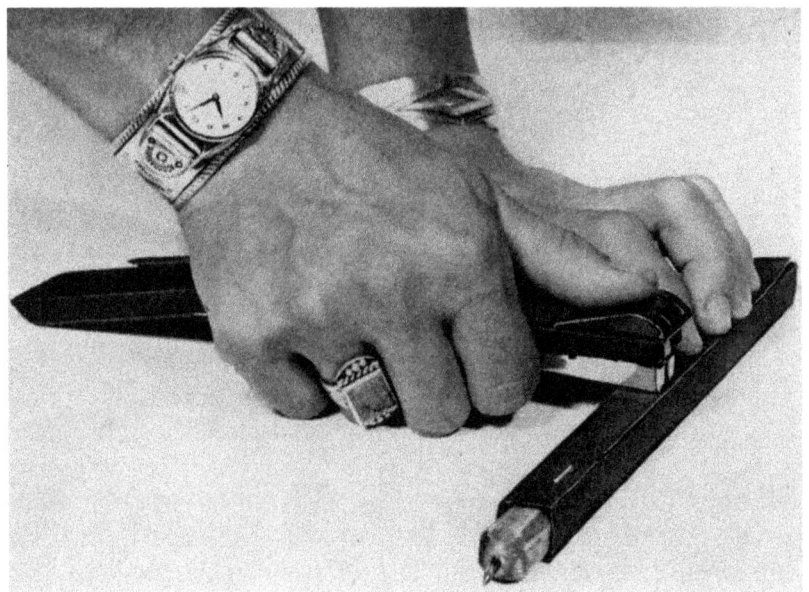

FIG. 70.   Stapling the last fold to stick

Importance of the Sketchbook

THE articles that have been shown are only a small percentage of what can be done in Indian silversmithing. For many years, the author has sketched and photographed pieces of Indian silver which he has seen. It has been found that sketching is the most practical method of recording, because in the sketch, details can be recorded that the camera cannot pick up. Plates 21, 22, and 31 show sketches made by the author.

To collect sketches or photographs of interesting pieces of Indian silversmithing, make a notebook about 5 by 8 in. Even though large stones are not available at the time, do not fail to sketch jewelry ornamented with stones.

Also be on the lookout for stamps, as there is no end of them and it is as much fun making them as it is using them. Always keep several sizes of tool steel on hand for making special stamps.

The Indian gets along with a minimum of tools, but he does so only from necessity. As it is in every field, the possession of good tools and enough of them makes almost any type of work a pleasure.

Supplies and equipment as well as catalogs may be obtained from dealers all over the country.

Index

Agatized wood, 49
Annealing frame, 45
Annealing steel, 15
Antiquing, 45
Anvils, 13
Appliqué work, 89
Arm guards, 109, 111

Beads, 140
Belt buckles, 80, 114, 116–119
Belt-buckle sets, 120-123
Belt endpieces, 118
Bench and tools, 10, 11
Bezels, 56, 58
Boutonnière vase, 151, 152
Boxes, 88, 91
Box-top designs, 88
Bracelets, hammered silver, 103–107, 110; sheet silver, 95–98
Brooches, 34, 73, 76, 77; butterfly, 127; dragonfly, 131; naturalistic and symbolic, 128
Buffing, hollow beads, 142; rings, 43
Bug pins, 135
Bumblebee pin, 133
Bump-ups, 118
Butterfly pin, 127, 133, 135
Button designs, 27
Buttons, concha, 25; Navaho, 28; stamping and filing, 26

Canteen tie clasp, 152
Channel bracelets, 70
Channel rings, 70
Channel work, 68–70
Chrysocolla, 46
Clasps for ear ornaments, 75
Concha belts, 78–80; old-style, 81
Concha buttons, 25
Cracked stones, 63
Cutting silver, 37
Cutting tools, 13

Dapping dies, 14, 19, 20
Dapping punches, 19
Dioptase, 46
Dragonfly brooch, 127, 130, 131
Drawing out ingots, 103

Ear ornaments, 71–73, 75
Emery stick, 154

Files, 14
Fitting turquoise for channel work, 69
Fluting, 97
Friendship rings, 39, 40, 43
Frog pin, 133

Grasshopper pin, 133, 135
Grinding turquoise, 51, 53

Hair clips, 32, 33
Half-round wire, 109
Hammers, 13
Hand polishing, 54
Heat for soldering, 13
Heating frame, 45
Hollow beads, 138, 140; buffing, 142; stringing, 145

Imitation cast bracelets, 106
Imitation cast rings, 65, 66
Indian-made rings, 61
Ingot molds, 103

Jeweler's rouge, 44
June-bug pin, 127

Katcina neckerchief slide, 87
Ketos, 109, 111, 112

Lapel pins, 34, 36, 133–135
Lap stick, 52
Malachite, 46
Men's rings, 66
Miniature canteen, 151, 152
Miniature vase, 151
Money clips, 30, 31, 33

Neckerchief slides, 82–87
Necklace pendants, 110

Pendants, 73, 110, 144, 145
Petrified wood, 49
Pickle bath, 38
Pickle jar, 14, 24
Pill boxes, 91

Pins, soldering, 35
Pliers, 14
Punches, 14

Raindrops, 21, 74
Removing stones, 64
Ring bands, 41
Ring blanks, 41
Ring designs, 62
Rings, 40, 41, 60; friendship, 39; Indian-made, 61; soldering, 41; without settings, 39
Rouge, 126

Saltcellars, 93, 94
Salt spoons, 93
Sandpaper stick, 54
Sawing silver, 34, 37
Setting, cracked turquoise, 64; stones, 58, 95; thin turquoise, 56
Silver, 23
Silver boxes, 90, 92
Silversmithing stamps, 16
Silver soldering, 19
Simulated turquoise, 69
Soldering, 44; canteen, 153; domes, 75; hollow beads, 142; pins and brooches, 37; raindrops, 44; squash blossoms, 142
Soldering equipment, 21

Soldering frame, 41, 45
Spoons, 93
Squash-blossom necklaces, 138, 139, 143
Squash blossoms, 73, 139, 142
Stamp boxes, 91
Stamp designs, 17
Stamping and filing buttons, 20
Stamps, 16, 71, 72
Stretching ring bands, 64
Stringing hollow beads, 145
Sulphuric acid pickle bath, 21
Sweating, 89

Tarnishing, 36, 45
Tea steeper, 124, 125
Tempering punches, 18
Tie clasps, 32, 33, 152; canteen, 152
Tools, 9
Triangular wire, forming, 106
Turquoise, 46; grinding, 53; polishing, 51; roughing out, 53
Turtle pin, 136, 137
Tweezers, 14
Twisting wire, 20

Vericite, 46

Workbench, 12
Wrist-watch bands, 146–149

About the Author

MASTER CRAFTSMAN and hobby expert with a nationwide reputation, W. "Ben" Hunt shares with all interested hobbyists the results of his experiences in silversmithing gained through association with many Indian tribes throughout the United States.

While Hunt is not of Indian blood, he has identified himself with the Indian mind through living with the Indians.

To acquaint himself with Indian lore, Hunt has traveled widely, visited pueblos and houses of the Southwest, the reservations of the Middle Western states, and of Canada. Living and camping with them, he has become so much their friend that they have given him an Indian name, "Tasunka Witko" which means Crazy Horse.

In his inner sanctum, a log cabin in the woods behind his home in Hales Corners, Wisconsin, Hunt develops the crafts that have been the subject matter of his many books. Besides his Indian name, Hunt is also known "Katcina Ben" to his Boy Scouts and many fans who admire the "katcinas," Indian dolls, that he is adept at carving.

Besides being a professional commercial artist, craftsman, lecturer, and author, Ben Hunt is a well-known Boy Scout leader and adviser. He regularly contributes articles on handicraft projects to professional and scouting magazines.

www.ingramcontent.com/pod-product-compliance
Lightning Source LLC
Chambersburg PA
CBHW040227180426
43200CB00026BA/2947